For A Season

Live · Learn · Grow

To

JENNY COOKE

YOU ARE SUCH AN AMAZING WOMAN
AND A ROLE MODEL TO ME. THANK
YOU FOR THE LOVE AND SUPPORT.
I WILL NOT DISAPPOINT. GOD BLESS

Rujeko Oscars - Brown

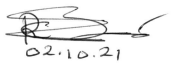

02.10.21

Cover Design
Sherman Baloyi
Onadsgn.com

Printed in Great Britain by
Biddles Books Limited, King's Lynn, Norfolk

Dedication

This book is dedicated to my late parents Oscar and Auxilia Katehwe who taught us to work hard and excel in life. I know that you are smiling from above with pride and joy, cheering me on. Your legacy lives forever.

Contents

Foreword

If you are going through a Season in your life where it feels like you are being tested, take some time to be still, and ask God how and when you should take action. As you turn the pages of For a season, you will find clarity, and gentle reassurance that what is happening within your Season is valuable, and that you will grow through the challenges you maybe facing.

One of the valuable lessons I have taken from Rujeko's story is that I am never alone, and there is a greater reason for everything that is happening within this Season of my life. When I tapped into this under-standing, my life started to gently fall back into place, and I was able to see the benefit of the delays I was experiencing. I was reminded that I was trying to do everything alone and had lost my connection to my source of inspiration.

Thank you Rujeko for reminding me and showing me that there is a greater purpose for the delays and lessons within this Season of my life. Today I can see things more clearly, and I know that I am being shown the way. You have shown me where I had lost my way and helped to restore my faith.

Open a page of For a Season, Live, Learn, Grow, and discover the message for your today.

Dawn Chrystal
Spiritual Life Coach
NLP and Bach Flower Remedy Practitioner
Reiki and Self -Help Author
Author – Divine Intervention and Free to be me.

Introduction

"It's only for a season...."

I had to keep reminding myself of this truth when I found myself homeless. *It was only for a season*; I kept telling myself, yet it did little to ease my fears as I had no idea how long this uncomfortable season would last. Yet, despite the discomfort and fear, the thought still gave me hope and strength to keep going on.

Slipping into homelessness is easier than you might think. We didn't realise this until we found ourselves without a home and all our possessions boxed and in storage. No one sits down to plan to be homeless. The possibility that we could become part of the homeless statistics never crossed my mind. How could it be? I had multiple degrees under my belt and a spouse of not-insignificant means. We had friends, relatives, and a network one expects to provide a safety net in times of trouble. Yet a series of unfortunate events would land me precisely there: A person of no fixed abode.

You never really think it can happen to you. Before this, I'd only heard of people losing their homes after failing to pay their mortgages due to being laid off from work or no longer able to afford the rentals because of serious illnesses or accidents. Or those who take financial risks at the wrong time and find themselves in a financial death spiral. I was aware of all this, but I never expected it could happen to my family and me. Many others have become homeless due to natural disasters or fires and circumstances out of their control. Again, I was very aware of this, but I never expected to become one of those statistics.

I'm sure we've all experienced seasons or a season in our lives where we've had to make painful sacrifices to accomplish our wishes and desires. We are a people that somehow expect our lives to sail smoothly, journeying through life with everything we need handed to us without any struggle, always triumphant. Unfortunately, life is not like that, nor is it the same for everyone. It is a challenging trek through peaks and valleys for most people, and yes, there is the fortunate bracket, on the other hand, to whom life is an easy sail. One thing that remains true is that life's journey is a long adventure and quest to fulfil one's dreams. God has a plan for every one of us. Until we understand the plan, we will wander in circles, and our lives will be like tangled spiderwebs, but with understanding, tenacity and faith on our part, God's plan for our lives can be fulfilled.

Birthing a vision

In 2020 my family went through one of the most unforgettable adventures of our lives when we sought to move up the property ladder. We discovered that getting to the finishing line was no easy feat; many detours characterised the road to achieving our goal.

We'd discussed the idea of moving houses a year before we started searching for a new home, but nothing concrete had come of it. Even though we knew we needed more space, we didn't pursue the idea until the end of that year. Little did we know that we positioned ourselves to what would become a house buying nightmare in the following year by procrastinating. We can now testify that getting to the finishing line is no easy feat; many detours, humps and roadblocks characterised the road we travelled to achieving our goal.

Life is a journey with many different paths; there are no wrong turnings, only paths we may not have known about and therefore didn't venture onto them. The decision to buy a house is not made within a day; neither is the process completed overnight. Buying a house is a significant investment, and things can quickly go wrong for the buyer if the parties (including professionals) do not adhere to the proper guidelines. From our nearly year-long journey, we have learnt that, for example, just as farmers do their due diligence and carry a business plan for their farming projects, the buyers and sellers in a house buying undertaking should do the same. I share our story in this book, where we were seeking to buy a house, and one of the crucial lessons we learned is that buyers must always weigh their options carefully, considering their financial circumstances in the process. And crucially, always expect that the unexpected might happen.

Our journey began when we decided to view a house a street away from ours. We set off with a verse from Exodus 33:14, *"My Presence will go with you, and I will give you rest."* (NIV). This was when God assured Moses that He would be with Him throughout the journey to set the children of Israel free. Our situation was different from Moses; however, we believed in Jehovah's promise to see us through every adventure in our lives. We held on to our faith and knowing that Yahweh was already in the plan, which brought us a sense of motivation and peace of mind. We needed to stay strong and determined for the journey ahead.

In most cases, the house buying process takes a while, from the planning stage to exchanging contracts and collecting the house keys. It can take from eight weeks to a year or more, depending on several issues, for example:

- A property may have obstacles to do with the seller not having all paperwork in place, or,

- it could be some delays in receiving the funds from the mortgage broker.

Whatever the issue, any holdups in processing the sale means that the process will take longer to complete. Sometimes the buyers or sellers may be in a chain where the next person fails to complete their sale in time. Parties involved must always provide the necessary information, whatever the cause of the delay. The grace to acquire a property can only locate us when we have done our part, allowing us to experience some peace throughout the journey.

Defining the phase

Have you ever been through a time in your life where you experience unbelievable things? Have you ever encountered one problem after another simply because you decided to start something good, something to better your life?

In life, we will go through some remarkable experiences, some good, others bad. I now understand that the time it took to buy our house was but a season. The Oxford dictionary describes a season as;

> *"The period or part of a year when something particular happens."*

It was a period of purchasing and moving into a bigger home for our family. It was the beginning of something beautiful in our lives, and we had many great expectations as we envisioned wonderful things coming out of this season. People make significant or minor changes during seasons, learning, growing, and trying to make the most of their time. The different activities in the different seasons demonstrate that there is a time for everything under the heavens. We should never take things for granted; everything happens for a reason and at the perfect time.

Seasons come and go; we must always be alert to discern the times. If the time is right, one can embark on a new project with much ease. If the time is not right, they will encounter obstacles that will affect their progress. In a planting season, farmers never anticipate cold snap, wilting plants or expect crops to wither. Farmers know the perfect time for planting and sowing every year. They know the times. Our lives are the same; everything happens at the right season.

Our Season

As we journeyed through the search for our perfect home, we discovered that everything took place in a cycle, one stage leading to the next. The cycle for home buyers runs as follows:

- Getting finances in place,
- Searching for the property,
- Viewing,
- Purchasing
- Moving in.

As with natural seasons, one cannot skip a stage to get to the next one; you must go through the process. Having said that, house buyers do not necessarily have to follow the natural seasons' calendar, but we can liken each stage of the buying process to a particular season. So, for example, you will know when your season for a change is about to start; you will experience unrest, a feeling that something needs to change.

Those who have bought properties will notice that how we handled our situation may differ from yours. However, I hope that you will learn something new from reading our story. Our house buying experience turned out to be a challenging experience mainly because of the Covid pandemic that hit not just us but the whole world in 2020, bringing everything to a halt. Unfortunately, we were caught unawares by many unforeseen complications that took us by surprise.

Having endured the process to the end, I can testify that it was not easy. I now know that many homebuyers are struggling due to some estate agents and Conveyancers' incompetence and lack of commitment. Many young couples and youths want to get on the property ladder, but they may not be privy to some issues. Not everyone will be able to survive the stress, pain and anxiety of waiting as we did.

I've always wanted to share my life's testimony, especially as I became a wife and mother, but this never happened. However, during the house buying journey, what we went through strengthened my resolve to share my story in a book. I hope our story will inspire more people to come out of their comfort zone to experience the goodness of God in their endeavours.

"For a Season, Live, Learn, Grow" narrates and discusses our house buying journey, starting from how we naively decided to purchase a house without a set plan and strategy in place. I narrate and discuss the obstacles we faced and eventually overcame during the nearly year-long experience. The book's essence is to provide you with vital knowledge required when embarking on any project, especially purchasing a house. I hope that my book will guide future home buyers to prepare well before looking for their new homes. I clearly outline some of the options we considered before searching or viewing. In addition, *For a Season – Live Learn Grow* also explores how we undertook to sort our finances and set a budget. Everything else after that became our story.

I take readers through some of the challenges we encountered as a family and how we finally came out with smiles on our faces. I discuss my attitude during this time as a child of God, sharing some of my most intimate moments with Jehovah. As a result, my faith grew. Therefore, instead of worrying, I was motivated and remained positive and resolute. Many Christians find it challenging to remain patient in adversity; I hope that as you read our story, you will learn how to find joy and peace amid a calamity. *"The Lord is good, a refuge in times of trouble. He cares for those who trust in Him." (Nahum 1:7, NIV).*

I have shared the coping strategies I used and hope these will encourage someone who may encounter the same or different trials and tribulations. In addition, I also share some summary quotes from each chapter to give readers some nuggets to take away. Finally, I pray that the message of this book, coupled with your effort and determination, will help you achieve your goals.

As much as the idea of buying a house may appear easy and give an exciting sense of accomplishment, we found that we needed God to walk the journey with us. Today, some Christians believe that they cannot share their financial aspirations with God, thinking they can accomplish such projects as house buying in their strength. Additionally, some may regard that house buying is straightforward and that Jehovah is not concerned about it, yet He is the source of all our strength (Nehemiah 8:10).

In *"For a Season: Live, Learn and Grow,"* I show how the Lord was in every aspect of the house buying process, including our lives, in a phenomenal way. His presence throughout this challenging journey demonstrates that we cannot achieve much without Him, but with His help, we can do extraordinary things (Isaiah 41:10). We can acquire, embrace, and advance with the Lord on our side no matter what trials we face.

I have attempted to show how we stood on the promises of the Lord in our homebuying episode, and I combine every experience with Bible verses for guidance. These were specific words that ministered to me and revealed that the Almighty was at work in our lives. It boosted my confidence and became the pillar on which I stood. Furthermore, they directed our thinking and acted as a light to the path to achieving our goal. How beautiful is it to look back and enjoy the success? My God is awesome, mighty in power and glorious in action.

May you be transformed in your mind, body and soul as you read this book; may you find some of the answers you are looking for.

May you be blessed,
Rujeko.

Chapter 1
A burning desire

A burning desire is the greatest motivator of every human action.

Paul. J Meyer

I stood to get my bible from the windowsill, and as I did so, it slipped and fell open onto the floor. Picking it up, I noticed that it had opened onto the book of Ecclesiastes 3, which reads: *"There is a time for everything and a season for every activity under the heavens."* What struck me most was verses 3 and 6, "a time to kill and a time to heal, a time to tear down and a time to build," "a time to search and a time to give up." I was amazed and thought, *wow, God does speak to us concerning the desires of our hearts;* He is concerned about all that concerns us.

It was a beautiful Saturday afternoon, and my family and I were sitting outside on the decking, enjoying the day while reflecting on how far we'd come in life. It had been a while since we'd shared such deep reflections, and despite everyone feeling a bit uncomfortable, we allowed each other time to say something about where they were and what they wished for in the future. Many people don't like going down memory for fear of encountering their past and facing the things they didn't do well. No one wants to look their disappointments and failures in the face. However, having these conversations is good practice as it clarifies where we stand in the present. And so, on that beautiful afternoon, we shared our thoughts despite feeling nervous and vulnerable; it was not a conversation to take lightly.

Earlier in the day, we'd discussed a house we'd viewed on the street next to ours. It had just come on the market, and on an impulse, we'd decided to go and view it. We had not as yet made a decision or shared

1

our thoughts concerning the house, but the questions we should have asked ourselves beforehand should have been:

- Is this the right time for us to buy?

- Have we set a budget aside?

- Do we know what type of house we want?

We should have done thorough research and obtained all the necessary information about the property, educating ourselves on what house buying entails. Once armed with the relevant information, we would then decide on how to move forward. Having the appropriate information provides the confidence to pursue your desires, and one can envision the impossible becoming possible. We, however, hadn't done any fact-finding research but rushed to view the house simply because it had come up on our dream street, Banbury Road. It dawned on us that we were now moving into a new season, as confirmed by the scripture in Ecclesiastes3.

People don't plan to fail; they fail to plan; we must understand that everything created was initially considered and planned. Even though our family was in a season, we needed to plan for it. Amongst the many issues discussed during Saturday's meeting was the burning desire to move into a bigger house; we needed space. There was now a real need to physically start to prepare for our dreams.

We all have different burning desires, as individuals or as family. For example, when I was twenty, I had a burning desire to become an air hostess, but the problem is that I didn't pursue this desire. A burning desire can be what you are highly interested in doing or becoming; it can also be a goal. Usually, with a burning desire, one can hope to accomplish all they seek to achieve no matter what it takes. From that burning desire, we gain the motivation and the strength to turn our goals into a reality. Without that push, we can never become who we want to be. Therefore, the desire should be a natural one, motivated from deep within.

The Seasons of Life

Our desires manifest through seasons. Different seasons make up our lives, and we must make every effort to understand these seasons and what they represent in our lives. There is no doubt that we live, learn, adapt and thrive in a specific period, and with this in mind, I felt reassured in my heart that the period we were entering was an exciting one. A shift in seasons can usher in new adventures and challenges that no one can anticipate in advance. Some seasons can be unsettling depending on how one responds to the obstacles that bring unnecessary demands to the fore. I felt that we were moving from the spring season of our lives into a summer season. Everyone had backed the idea of going ahead with looking for a house to buy.

Natural seasons come in cycles of cold winters, hot summers, planting season and harvest time. We all go through good or bad seasons. Our seasons are also cyclic as children of God, where we experience growth, stagnation, or lack. Just as the earth displays and speaks through the different seasons, God speaks, conveying His heart during the seasons of our lives.

Our year in the UK is divided into four seasons, summer, autumn, winter and spring; it's cyclical and influenced by the rotation of our position on the earth to the sun. From June to August, the country's position is tilted towards the sun and receives more heat. In these summer months, people start to harvest what they planted in spring; however, it can still rain and sometimes floods occur.

Many celebrations like festivals, parties, weddings, and graduations occur in summer because of the excellent weather, and many people can get out. On the other hand, the northern solstice reminds us to focus on tending and guarding the crops we seeded; these can be plants growing in the garden or fields. It is not time to sit back, as we can still sow more crops depending on their characteristics.

In the life of Christian believers, the summer season is a period of receiving, rejoicing and celebrating blessings from our Father in Heaven as we watch our gifts growing and manifesting the glory of our creator. God has a plan to prosper each of us (Jeremiah 29:11). In our summer months, Yahweh's ideas manifest, the ideas hatch, and we get to use everything God prepared for us in His plan. Our purpose is derived from this position, and we can take action as it is a season of productivity. We must develop and enjoy our vision because we can experience success and positively influence our communities when this is managed well. Still, we mustn't forget that during some seasons, we thrive, while in others, we survive; life occurs in seasons.

I realised that all along, we had been enjoying the benefits brought in by the spring seasons of our lives and that it was now time to take action if we were to bring in a harvest in the summertime. All things being equal, it was going to be a remarkable season for us. For many, summertime is inspiring and exciting because we witness seeds sown in previous seasons come to maturity and celebrate the harvest. If we consider the planning stages, this season would be classed as a time of goal achievement for us; everything we'd planned coming to manifestation. Of course, seasons are not the same for everyone. For other people, some summers are barren, characterised by dry spells despite having worked hard with an expectation to reap a good harvest, but it doesn't happen. They may have failed to plan according to the seasons, and their projects fail to succeed. When we realise that we have failed to secure a successful harvest, we should revisit our plans; we still can change the course of action or amend the existing plans. All this takes place when we have that deep, burning desire to achieve something.

We travelled a difficult road, but the Bible reminded us to remain steadfast despite the drought season, with our eyes fixed on God. So we sat tight, holding onto what His lasting promises bring during the different seasons. Our God is always with us, whatever stage of life we find ourselves.

The Autumn season commences in September and runs through to November; it starts getting chilly, and the days get shorter with long nights. We get less sunshine, signalling the last phase of the harvesting season for specific crops. However, we can still enjoy the last traces of sunshine, and some people still take holidays in early Autumn with parties still carrying on.

For Christians, Autumn provides an opportunity to take ownership of everything that happened in the summer. Our prayer results carry us through as we keep rejoicing and recognising the joys brought in by our yields. Whatever fruits we harvest, we know they are an outcome of our planting. Even as we continue to celebrate, we should not forget that Autumn is not permanent or any other season. We must remember to keep our harvest seed because it determines our preparedness for the next season.

From December to February, we have the Winter season; these are the coolest months of the year, where we experience shorter days with darker nights. Depending on the outlook for that calendar year, we may also get storms and lots of wet wintry weather. Some winters are a combination of cold, wet, calmer weather with lots of snow, fog and frost. On the other hand, some spells have a harsh, bitter winter throughout.

We have to prepare ahead for such a harsh season or adjust and manage it well. Winter is not a season for sowing because it is wet throughout. Instead, it can be a season for reflection and resting. Even if one desired to sow any seeds, one would have to wait for the right time. To achieve success, we must plan; therefore, we can use the winter months for drafting or redrafting our action plans. Where redrafting is not possible, we can realign our steps to amend some of our tasks. Ezra (10:4) encourages us to rise, for the matter is in our hands. There is always support if we need it; we must not stop taking action in any season. What we need is the courage to take the required steps. We must not procrastinate when we have a burning desire but act on it, regardless of the season.

In our Christian walk, we are taught to appreciate the night times, which are different from the daytime. Sometimes we face personal winters that destroy us. Our disappointments depend on how we handle the cold winters of life that can affect our careers and relationships. Despite the disappointments, it is a time to be strong and keep forging ahead. Instead of complaining about the experiences, we can harness the downtime to prepare for our Spring. We keep going and look forward to the clocks moving ahead again. But, don't forget that winter only lasts for a few months; it's only for a season. Time is constantly moving, and our understanding of the times brings commitment into every activity in every season.

The Spring season is from March to May, with a much welcome massive shift from the cold winter. The days start getting longer and warmer, and there is a sense of nature coming awake. Some trees get fresh buds; others, like the cherry blossom, will flower, whilst the first daffodil flowers. Notwithstanding, birds like the bald eagle, the hairy woodpecker and the red-tailed hawk build their nests. We also get busy, a time for taking advantage of the opportunity in our midst. Our ability to embrace the moment can be portrayed by how resourceful we become.

> *"Opportunity follows struggle. It follows effort. It follows hard work. It doesn't come before."*
> SHELBY STEELE

The winter hardships are an opening for new beginnings. We can lay claim to the perfect job of acknowledging the Spring season without making excuses. My late mother always encouraged us to seize the opportunities in Spring and not let the weather confuse us. The key to our success is never to procrastinate but to take action today. As much as springtime brings changes, we can embrace them by taking action. When one has a burning desire, there comes a need to take action immediately. I love the words of Aeschylus, who said that time brings all things to pass. Spring is a time to plant seeds; therefore, we try not to miss the opportunity to plant.

Each moment is an opportunity. If we start planting today, we can either become good at planting or miss out on gaining the skills. However, we must remain alert even in this season as sometimes we can sow the wrong seeds and produce a bad harvest. We always must face the risk that not all good seeds produce a good harvest, and not all bad seeds will produce a bad harvest. There are always lessons to learn from every decision we make.

Some seasons are for blessings, whilst others are for toiling. Our family had no idea of the season we were entering; it was a brand-new season. We had to be careful as sometimes we have looked at those in wintertime and said negative things about them, but in no time they come out of their winter season. We needed to seriously address this attitude, as we soon realised that we were blocking our progress. Our negative thoughts were coming to fruition in ways that were not helpful or productive to achieving our desired outcome.

The reverse can be true for those experiencing a summer season. Those experiencing Spring may rejoice as if they are in summer. Seasons present themselves at different times and in different ways for different people; we experience them differently. In the Bible, Isaac sowed seeds during a dry season, and his harvest was plentiful. So likewise, our God can ask us to sow during a drought because He knows we can reap in any season when we walk with Him. When we sow a seed, we expect to harvest, and as such, I always pray for God to grant us wisdom to know what to do in every season.

Make informed decisions

After viewing the house on Banbury Road, my daughter and I were drawn to it; it ignited a burning desire in us and opened our eyes to what could be ours. The burning desire fuelled us, and we were excited; however, my husband Richard didn't share the same excitement. He was not prepared to jump in without checking out our finances first. During the past few years, we had worked hard and saved some money; one of our joint desires was to upgrade to a larger, more comfortable home that could accommodate our needs for space and privacy.

Our conversations that afternoon expounded further on the details; moving to a bigger house would solve the lack of space in our current home. It had become so crowded with belongings that there was no extra space for studying, relaxation or family gatherings. We also needed a bigger garden to grow vegetables as well as hosting family and friends. In addition, we wanted to be in a desirable location. We, of course, knew it would all come at a cost financially. There would also be other risks and practical details to take care of; we first needed to look into all these issues.

Whilst we were still discussing, a phone call came through from the estate agent asking for our thoughts regarding the house we'd viewed. Following a short conversation, we concluded that the viewing was a starting point for us as we needed to test the waters. Once we decided on what we desired, we had to take the first step, which can be a milestone for many. However, many people find it hard to start anything even when there is nothing specific holding them back, and this is why we have many people with ideas they have been talking about for years. They have done nothing to explore, nor understand their idea better, to enable them to decide on what action to take.

I needed to convince Richard that it was the right time to purchase a house. I understood that buying a house was one of life's most important decisions, which for most, is a one-off. The time to make that decision was here, and I was looking at getting a family home that we would enjoy through to retirement, God willing. We agreed to engage an independent financial advisor to confirm our financial obligations and ability to afford the purchase. I did not want to rely on the advice of people who were not qualified and experienced in financial matters. The decision to allow other people's opinions and suggestions to influence our goals lies with us. With the correct information, we can make our goals into reality; we can then rise with courage and take the necessary next steps to change our lives.

The word of God encourages us to follow good biblical economics, that as couples, we must not get into unnecessary debt. Likewise, we must be free from slavery to selfishness and indebtedness. Proverbs 22:7 warns that the rich rule over the poor and the borrower is a slave to the lender. If we borrow unnecessarily as a couple, we can become servants to the lender and remain at their mercy should we struggle to clear the debts. These are some of the principles I needed to remind Richard in case he had forgotten. God has been keeping His financial promises to us; we have never lacked anything. We were not that materialistic, and we did our best to support the church. We always carried our financial planning based on our cash flow, not our dreams; that was the principle we adopted from the beginning of our marriage. The Word of God also promises that He will never leave nor forsake us; we knew we were not alone (Hebrews 13:5). Thus, contacting a financial adviser would help us brainstorm, plan and decide how much we could spend on a new family home. After that, we could then set realistic goals for the process.

Within the following week, I had made an appointment with a financial adviser we had known for some years. The meeting helped us to appropriate funds as we already had a positive cash flow. Richard was pleased with the outcome, acknowledging that we could go ahead. By the time we left, we had a budget. The clarity on what one desires acts as a green light to go after one's dreams. In addition, we had to make sure that our goals were smart enough to be executed and finally, with a good budget, we could get things moving. Finally, we had to stay positive, knowing nothing could stop us with everything in place.

We realised we had to make important decisions about this house, but not just that, as children of God, we turned to the Almighty and His Word, discerning that we could not leave Him out of the process. Yahweh is the one who gives us good gifts because everything belongs to Him (James 1:17). Turning to the Creator activates Him to take control of the process, to guide and lead us. His Word says, "Build houses and settle down; plant gardens and eat what they produce" (Jeremiah 29:5, NIV).

So, then we set out to find a house that met all our criteria, that would bring joy to our family, a house that would prosper and propel us. Above all, a house that God would give us according to His plans. Further to understanding God's word, we prayed and committed everything into God's hands.

Takeaway Nuggets

1. Daily reflections are powerful.

2. Discuss your failures, talk about your successes.

3. A plan follows a burning desire.

4. Life has it that we move from one season to the next.

5. Never take any season for granted.

6. Everything we plan will come to pass when we act.

7. Engage others to appraise your plan.

Chapter 2

The Journey Begins

A journey of a thousand miles begins with a single step.

Lao Tzu

Ding dong! Ding dong, the doorbell rang early on Friday morning. I checked the time from the comfort of my duvet and realised it was already 8 am. Richard jumped out of bed to answer the doorbell, and it was the removal team. It was time to leave our old home on Providence Green, and we'd been packing all day and night, retiring to bed in the early hours of the morning of the 29th of February 2020. It wasn't exactly the best day for moving, weather-wise; it was raining cats and dogs! We'd done our best to pack, but the house was still half full, and we had run out of boxes. The arrival of the removal van brought much relief as we were grateful for the added help. However, we needed to avoid further stress and anxiety by getting ourselves organised and remaining calm to make progress.

Looking back, since our offer on the property we wanted was accepted in mid-October 2019, moving things forward had been a nightmare. We wanted to move into the new house by Christmas because my sister and her family were coming to spend the holidays with us. However, the initial searches on the house revealed that the house had over seven loans attached to it and these needed clearing quickly if we were going to make it for Christmas. We loved the house so much; we went ahead with the purchase. In hindsight, we really should have taken the time to consider the risk factors involved in proceeding with a property with such issues. We prayed that God would make it possible for us to move into the property as soon as possible.

Stay calm and do something

Nothing much happened until mid-December when our conveyancing team updated us that there were still four debts remaining. We tried to communicate with the estate agent, but there was not much progress going on. We learned that the couple was in the process of divorcing and had both moved out. It became clear that nothing would happen quickly. We, therefore, started preparing to spend Christmas in our home despite having started packing. Unfortunately, it was too late to cancel my sister's visit as they had made plans ahead of time.

Consequently, we had one of the worst Christmases ever in 2019, with boxes in every corner of the house, but despite all that, we remained positive. We needed to think and remain positive to manage the situation we found ourselves in, and we looked forward to moving out as soon as possible. We received news that only one debt was remaining against our new home by the end of January, which brought a huge sigh of relief. The news was a good sign, and we began to think that we would be moving soon; a positive mindset is everything.

> *"Instead of worrying about what you cannot control, shift your energy to what you can create."*
>
> ROY BENNET

I had been shopping from the January sales for some of the light fixtures we would need in the new home; we believed we would most likely move into the new home by the end of February, going by the conveyancer's estimation. So shopping was part of preparing for the new season of moving to our new home. We discovered that preparing kept us busy, and we worried less about the move.

"I will prepare. Someday my chance will come," these words by Abraham Lincoln encouraged and motivated us to do likewise. Getting ready for the next move was needed. From the solicitor's estimation, we would most likely move into the new home by the end of February. Jimmy Carter encourages Christians to live lives as if Jesus Christ was

coming that very afternoon; we should be ready in heart, soul, and mind to go with Christ at any given moment. Therefore, we didn't want to leave it too late, only to pack under pressure or rush in the last hour. Luke warns that "You must be ready for the son of man is coming at an hour you do not expect." (Luke 12:40, NIV). Getting ready means that we have to trust the process. We can only do that by thinking ahead, which is what we were trying to do. Moving would be less of a rush if we were to wake up and hear the good news of completion.

By mid-February, the situation had not changed, and we were getting anxious about what could happen. It was not very clear what the next step was with the purchase. What became apparent was that we had to move from our house by the end of the month; our house had found new owners. After chatting with the conveyancers, we sat down as a family one evening to plan what to do next. It was a stressful evening as we couldn't develop a solution; we were all worried about the coming days. No one knew what lay ahead or how long it would take to resolve.

Never look down on yourself

Following a conversation with one of our friends, they surprised us by offering us the opportunity to move in with them until we had a house. This was a wonderful surprise! We never expected anything like this. Angels come within the darkest hours. Putting the phone down, I felt better having spoken to someone. I realised sometimes we need a listening ear. If we keep things to ourselves, they become more burdensome; however, finding someone to talk to about what you are experiencing may be helpful. It's even much better when they provide meaningful advice.

Hoping that we would soon be moving into our own home, we acquired some storage space for our furniture and other belongings and moved in with our friends who lived 7 miles away. We needed to be out of the house by 2 pm, but it took longer than expected, and the process was depressing. We finally left at 6 pm, when the next occupants were waiting outside in their van. It was a painful way to leave a place we'd loved and have been comfortable in for the past five years.

One of the prayers we made at the beginning of the house buying process was that we wouldn't end up with a house not meant for us. We, therefore, asked Jehovah to close every door to houses that were not meant for us and open the doors for the right one. When the sellers accepted our offer, we got excited; it was a miracle! Yahweh had answered our prayers, making us believe that He had a plan for us in this house. Psalm 127:1(NIV), confirms that the Godhead is the builder of every home; without Him, we labour in vain. We believed that God had answered our prayers, and hence, everything throughout the process would be a thanksgiving. God's omnipresence would sustain us in every step of the purchase. Moving out of our home to stay with friends was the next step in this journey; there was a glimmer of hope. Our prayer focus changed once it became apparent that we were leaving our house.; we prayed for direction for the next step.

Once we moved into our friends' house, things took a turn for the worst when in the second week of March, it emerged that there were Corona Virus cases in the country. Safety regulations had to be adhered to, constant sanitising, wearing masks and social distancing. Our anxiety and stress levels reached the roof; we had no idea what would happen if things did not change. Every day, I was on the phone checking on the progress of the house, but no news came from the estate agent and the conveyancers. The whole situation seemed hopeless, ushering in a rollercoaster of emotions in all of us. Quite often when we are caught in a situation it is hard to understand what is going on. However, the best we can do for ourselves is to accept what has happened and work on how we feel.

Take action; keep trusting

As we struggled to figure out our next move, the country headed for a national lockdown due to the spread of COVID-19. Everything changed completely as we all struggled to figure out how to take precautions to protect ourselves and each other. We'd been at our friends' house for over two weeks by this time, and they had a right to know what our plans were. It was a time of uncertainty for all of us. We also, of course, missed being in our own space, and we, therefore, decided to start looking for a house to rent.

I look up to the mountains; where does my help comes from? (Psalm 121:1NIV). I can imagine what sort of situation David was in when he wrote this psalm. There were times when we felt we had nowhere to look except to God and sometimes, situations force us to throw ourselves into action. Once we realised, we couldn't procrastinate anymore, we decided to take action. Jim Rohm said, *"every action we take starts a new cycle in our lives".* So we decided to start looking for a house to rent. We went to view a flat in the next town and on the way, we passed through a friend's house for packing boxes. It never crossed our minds that she would turn out to be an angel sent by God.

The flat we viewed was lovely, but the Landlord was still decorating it. The landlord promised to do his best to move us in within the next three days. That meant we had to wait at our friends' house for the next 48 hours. Still, we had a decision to make concerning the flat because the minimum rental period was six months. We still didn't have a clear picture of the situation with our house. What we discovered was that it was hard to get a short-term rental property. Even if they were available, the market at that time didn't have anything to meet our criteria. While waiting for news about the rental flat, the friend we'd collected boxes from rang the following evening and chipped in to accommodate us till we moved to our house. She thought it would be better for us to stay with her instead of renting a property. Still, we all thought this arrangement would be for a couple of weeks; we never knew the Coronavirus pandemic was just starting and would be there for a while. As we were moving to the friend's house, the Prime Minister announced the national lockdown. The estate agent told us they could not proceed with our rental application as they were now following government guidance and closing; this was another nail in the house buying coffin.

The story of Naomi in the Bible teaches that things can go wrong. Naomi and her husband Elimelech left Bethlehem to become immigrants in Moab. (Ruth 1:1-22 NIV). They were looking for a better life as there was a famine in their homeland; they hoped everything would go well for them. Instead of prospering, things went very wrong; Naomi lost her husband together with her two sons. She found herself a widow with no children or grandchildren. That was a double loss, a crisis that made her choose to go back to her homeland. When things go wrong, we are left with many questions that we cannot answer in most cases. Similarly, as Christians, we sometimes ask Yahweh many questions when we face challenges.

Some of the questions I asked God were:

- Why didn't we see this coming, yet we were praying?
- Where are you in this Lord?
- What's next?
- How can we come out from this?

It was hard to believe that we'd had a house of our own not long before, but within a short space of time, we were homeless and temporarily staying with friends. It was difficult to imagine that we didn't have a house anymore; we had lost our peace and independence. It happened so quickly, and we never saw it coming? How had we not seen this coming?

I had never in all my life thought that I would be moving into someone else's house because I had no home of my own. I felt that our situation taught us to remain humble and gentle, patient and bearing with one another in love (Ephesians 4:2). I never imagined that I would live with friends without knowing what the next step in my life looked like. Now that we were here, we believed that God wanted us to count our blessings. We were not where we were because we were poor, but a situation had gone out of control.

"Nothing in life is permanent, be humble."

ANONYMOUS

The Bible in Isaiah 55:8 says, *"For my thoughts are not your thoughts, neither are your ways my ways."* (NIV). We all want things to go our way but looking at where we were; we felt the Lord wanted us to trust Him with every plan concerning our lives. Instead of focusing on the details of our plans and expecting them to come to pass just like that, we should look to God, who says He will reveal His hand upon everything that we set out to do. We should trust the Almighty once we have involved Him in our projects.

It does not matter what course the plans we take follow; we should never lose focus. In our case, we had expected to move into our house within 6-8 weeks as confirmed by the conveyancers; however, ten weeks later, there was no sign of any contracts exchanging. Having planned, expected, and acted, we were proved wrong. It was only our plans, not God's plans; we should have involved and consulted Him. As Christians, we must understand that our plans may not materialise, and this can cause many disappointments. We should never be angry with God because our plans did not go the way we wanted; instead, we should continue to look to Him and expect Him to fulfil His plan in our lives. Not only will the Creator do it alone, but we also owe Him the responsibility to act and look at all options available.

Looking back, we had not made any allowances for delays or difficulties that may arise in the process. We had not taken time to reflect on the situation and discern what God was saying to us at every stage. Instead, we focused on how we wanted to come out of the plan. We learned that in every programme, there is a purpose to be fulfilled.

God's intention through the delay was to teach us tolerance in everything as His children. Whatever we plan with Him, His thoughts and strategy regarding our situation may differ from what we think. So being patient is an act of giving Jehovah a chance to fulfil His perfect intentions for our situation. Once we remain steadfast, we must not anticipate God's actions and tell him what to do when things don't work out. Joyce Meyer sums it best in her book "Never Give Up" when she advises us to learn to trust God, the One who knows all things.

Living with friends highlighted that we should never take anything for granted. Having a home is a privilege; no one chooses or wishes to be homeless. As time went on, we realised that we were just like any other person who had been homeless. We were not superior in any way, neither were we the only family who deserved better. We don't always have to wallow in self-pity in times of affliction; we needed to pick ourselves up and stay strong during the trying times. God works through faith, hope and expectation. Sometimes our Creator will send angels to help us; we never know who will come through for us in our time of need.

Takeaway Nuggets

1. Stay committed to your goal.

2. Watch out for stress and anxiety; life's disruptions are quick to invite stress.

3. Act don't procrastinate.

4. You have the tools within you.

5. Accept help from other sources.

6. Trust the all-knowing power; God knows it all.

7. Every life event requires our preparation.

Chapter 3

Searching and viewing

If you haven't found it yet, keep looking.

STEVE JOBS

Searching for a home is eye-opening; it is the pivotal part of the house buying exercise that you cannot afford to get wrong. It can be daunting yet exciting at the same time. The meeting with the financial advisor gave us the confidence we needed to proceed with our desire to buy a house. Choosing a location was not much of a problem as we didn't want to move too far from where we currently lived. We were comfortable with the area, given its proximity to most amenities, and most houses on the estate had generous rooms. Homestratosphere, a leading website that covers everything home related, encourages buying a house far enough out of the city where the traffic isn't heavy but close enough to the city that pizza delivery is possible.

Although there weren't many new houses in the area, there were a few new developments. We noted that most newly built houses in the area had small rooms and tiny gardens, which did not lend themselves well to us. In addition to this, my husband had always been against newly built properties. I don't blame him for that; he had his reasons. Richard's previous experiences of buying houses must have taught him lessons he would not easily forget. There will always be lessons to learn in any undertaking, but we should not make the same mistakes as before.

"A clear vision backed by definite plans gives a tremendous feeling of confidence and personal power." Brian Tracy. Clarity of vision is one of the most critical steps to greatness. For example, when buying a house, it is essential to be clear about what one is looking for from the onset. Being clear about the type of house we were going to buy was necessary.

We gained some knowledge from reading about modern property development on information sites which confirmed our thoughts. Most developments offered different types of houses, from flats to detached properties within the same streets, but we decided that newly constructed homes were not an option. Our focus was mainly on resale homes within our neighbourhood, although our list excluded properties three miles outside our current location.

Consider all options

When planning for a house purchase, we are encouraged to consider all the options available equally. However, it can be a daunting time, especially when there aren't that many options available. With the prevailing state of the economy, it can be expensive for most home buyers to give someone else the task of finding a home for them. Engaging an estate agent to help us with the property search was not a priority, given that our financial advisor had already pointed out some tips for us. We considered that commissioning one would be an unjustified expense, although they probably would do a good job.

During our family discussion, we agreed that Estate agents were more interested in representing their interest than the buyer because they worked on commission. We had previously used an Estate agent to look for a house to rent, and we felt that they had pushed us to agree for a let that was more in their best interests than ours. As a result, we didn't even consider the idea in the present circumstances, and this is where we got it all wrong. It would have been acceptable if we had not done it due to lack of finances, but our reason was that it would be expensive.

Part of our preparation was to educate ourselves on where to extend our searches on the market, the areas to focus on, and estate agents to consider visiting for enquiries. We compiled a list of questions to ask the vendor, including an offer for a prospective house. That being the case, we felt we'd covered our ground. However, we later realised we had not prepared well for what lay ahead of us when we stepped out to look for our dream home. Although our list was not guaranteed to get us the best house, we tried to develop the right, factual questions to obtain a genuine standing. Our checklist did not have a massive list of things. Some of the questions we drafted included the following:

- Has the seller had any offers? If so, how many?
- What was the seller's reason for selling or moving?
- Have they made some house improvements or renovations? What are they?
- What are their annual expenditures on water, gas and electricity?
- What is the council tax band of the property?

Due to work commitments, we agreed to view properties at weekends when we were all at home, including our daughter, who was at university during the week. We scheduled appointments across the day, mostly midday or just before, to get the best possible view. Our search began in February 2019, it was springtime, and we hoped it would be good timing to find the right house within a reasonable time. Springtime is a season of new beginnings as the earth reverts to life after the cold winter season. On the ground, new buds come through and begin to bloom. Farmers will start to execute their yearly plans by planting new seeds. It is a busy season for them, sometimes working non-stop, from early morning and finishing before midnight. They must do this before the wintertime comes; this is crucial to set new crops for a bountiful harvest in the following season.

The coming of springtime in the UK triggers the temperatures to rise slowly, although there may be some variations based on location. Christians view springtime as a period of sowing good deeds; there is plenty in storehouses; therefore, there is plenty to give and bless others. In Proverbs 3:27, we are encouraged not to withhold good from whom it is due, when it is in our power to act. This season resonated well with us as a family, and we believed things would go well for us.

View and observe feedback

A viewing provides an opportunity to dig deeper into the property's circumstances; therefore, every buyer should do their best to leave no stone unturned. We started by viewing five properties one weekend and learned that we needed to be thorough with each viewing. Out of the five we viewed, only two fit the criteria on our list, so we set to book more viewings.

Within the first batch of houses viewed, we discovered that most of them did not match the descriptions provided in the advertisements. Sometimes estate agents would provide misleading information, especially in house photographs. For example, some pictures reflected a big garden or kitchen, which was not always the case upon viewing. Other houses would look very small on paper, yet upon viewing, the opposite was true. Another example was a house close to the road with no parking space, but the photograph depicted a different picture. In such an instance, we would have to consider its future potential, i.e., potential for renovations. We had to get second or third viewings for a house with potential before submitting an offer if it met our criteria. We needed to be careful with price negotiations for such properties. We were left confused; we'd had such high expectations when we set out to go viewing. Consequently, we learnt to have an open mind and expect anything with each house we viewed.

Being close to almost all amenities was one of our priorities. For a dream home, having access to all amenities is gratifying. My husband and I enjoy outdoor activities; therefore, some of the amenities we considered were recreation parks or running trails nearby. Even though we both drive, access to shops was always an added advantage for us. We learned that seeing beyond the property is possible when a buyer has the seller's cooperation in providing relevant information.

We had an instance where the estate agent arranged to meet their colleague at a house we wanted to view. Whilst viewing, we asked questions about certain specifics of the house and discovered she didn't have adequate information, promising to get back with the answers later in the day. This did not make sense as one of the questions was a simple one about which schools were close to the property. She confessed she didn't know much about the house as she was only a university student working part-time during weekends. As if this was not enough, we were accompanied to another viewing by a retired policeman from a different estate agent the following weekend. Whilst talking about the boiler, he pointed out that he would hand it over to the estate agent as he was doing views part-time. It became apparent that we had to be careful with viewings at weekends as in many cases estate agents sent trainees or inexperienced colleagues. Where they didn't have information, no follow up was made from the office to explain. We were disappointed as this caused delays to our search.

At one point, the estate agent representative did not show up on time, and we had to wait outside in the rain. Nobody called to make us aware of the delay, and so we drove back home. In hindsight, we should have realised these were some of the red flags about the incompetence of some estate agents. We also observed that sometimes the sellers were not entirely helpful in some of the viewings; they could not provide adequate answers when asked how certain things work. This was mainly with Council tax bills, covenants or services operations, and any problems or plans with the local area. Eventually, we thought perhaps we could have set our priorities right about which estate agents to use from the onset. At other times, there were no answers to basic questions, like how long the current occupants had lived in the house. We resolved that we needed to go the extra mile to get as much information as possible from a seller or representative. Estate agents need to possess specialist knowledge on each property they are selling or leave it to the owner to provide the correct information.

Dig Deeper

"To buy a home is to buy a better way of life."
HOMESTRATOSPHERE

We must never forget to take personal responsibility for our lives and the future that we desire. Everyone who embarks on this journey must do what it takes to achieve a better way of life. There is a story in the Bible about the wise and foolish builders (Luke 6:46-49). The wise man dug his foundations deep and laid them on the rock. The house was not shaken by the torrential storms when the floods came because it was well constructed. On the other hand, the foolish man built his house on sand without laying any foundation. When the rains came, with a huge rainstorm, it struck the house, destroying it.

"If you include God in the decisions you make about purchasing your new home, He will not fail to show up and bless you."
ANONYMOUS

We must be careful about the information we collect and the choices we make concerning prospective houses. Our failure to obtain adequate information will cause destruction or end in serious regrets. For example, we needed a house with enough space for various reasons. We, therefore, should always seek God's counsel during the process to help us find a perfect location, size, and structure.

Some houses had high asking prices, yet their structures didn't match the price. It was apparent that the Estate agent or the owner may have allowed for a broader negotiation. In some cases, a property in a popular area showed a great need for modernisation, yet the selling price would not reflect the enormity of the work to be done. Usually, such houses are in desirable locations, and this would call for serious negotiations on the price based on the work to be done.

For example, on a particular viewing, the house needed a complete renovation. The estate agent told us there was planning permission to extend the kitchen and bathroom. We viewed the house; however, between us, none of us had done renovation work before, neither did we know any builders. We, therefore, decided that it was not the best house for us. In another house, the owners were selling furnishings separate from the house. This included soft furnishings, a fixed cooker, and security cameras fixed to the house, things they couldn't take with them if we didn't need them. So, again, it was something we had never come across; we started to consider other options.

The viewing of new houses was well organised in our catchment area, as a representative usually carried it out for the developer whose offices were onsite. We had our best experience viewing newly built homes as they don't usually have any issues. However, we found them to have small rooms that we could not compromise on, although the house plans were beautiful. Some new developments had houses built by individuals who had bought land from the developer, and this was something new to us. Upon viewing one of the houses on the new estate, we realise the seller had built the house using mainly cheap materials. As a result, the kitchen's quality was substandard compared to the rest of the estate. However, it was comforting to know that we had been made aware by the developer that they had nothing to do with that house; therefore, it was up to us to view or not. We eventually decided to forget about pursuing newly builds and concentrate on houses built between 15-25 years ago. They appeared to be ticking most of our boxes in terms of space. Throughout all our viewings, we prayed for guidance on choosing the right house.

Some properties needed cosmetic updating, which could either be redecorating or putting in new carpets. We didn't mind that if we liked the property. It took us from March till August to find a house that ticked most of our boxes. It came on the market after a dry spell between the last week of August to mid-September when there was nothing at all on the market. God came through for us; we even found favour with the vendor who chose to negotiate with us. We felt convinced this was a property God wanted our family to have. We didn't see anything coming; however, we have learned that one can swim or sink with faith. We chose to swim. While submitting the paperwork, some unforeseen circumstances occurred, and we lost the house. Even though this was beyond our control, it was still a hard blow to take. We went back on the market, searching with high hopes.

Towards the end of October, we finally got a property in a location we had not even looked at before as we thought we couldn't afford it. God opened that door for a slightly cheaper property that needed some cosmetic work. Although minimal, we felt convinced that the work required would give us an excellent renovating experience. At the same time, what excited us was that our budget allowed us to carry out decent improvements without stress and still leave a bit of money for new furniture. We loved that we could live in the house while doing it up, a bonus for us. Finding this property marked the beginning of exciting times ahead; little did we know the house was a ticking time bomb waiting to explode.

The initial searches revealed that the property had up to seven debts attached to it. The estate agent assured us they were working on it; apparently, this was usually not a problem to sort out. However, reality finally hit when we realised, we had to vacate our house at the end of February 2020 to accommodate the new tenants. We realised the enormity of the debts on the house and how complex the case had turned out to be. We'd assumed that the professionals were collaborating all this time, making sure we moved from our old house into the new property. Instead, we were alerted to some of the ordeals people come across in property buying. We had to make arrangements for our accommodation and storage for belongings.

Searching during the pandemic

Once we moved to stay with friends, the country went into lockdown due to the Covid pandemic, and the house purchase process had to halt. It was a challenging time for us all. Our conveyancers had not set a plan for working out of office, and We couldn't do much about it; the situation was affecting everyone. The person we dealt with from the seller's estate agent left the company, and the agency did not replace him due to the Covid situation. This season tested our faith, and we had to remember that having faith gives room for God's will to be fulfilled, and we needed that for the days ahead. At the beginning of June 2020, the lockdown lifted, and in our excitement, we quickly contacted the conveyancers only to be told that they were still waiting to hear from the sellers' solicitors. At this point, we were losing patience and came up with plan B. Many people advised us to abandon the property, but we had fallen in love with it. At the same time, God was not saying anything concerning our next move; therefore, we decided to wait. We started searching for another house whilst we waited for the original property to complete. This time we were searching in areas we had not included in our original checklist.

At one point, we went to view two different properties in a village about five miles away. These were beautiful houses, one of which was out of our budget. We enjoyed viewing these village homes; they came with large rooms, quiet cul-de-sac and many extras, including large gardens. We had no issues buying a house outside our catchment area, but we were worried about the availability of transport for our daughter, who commuted to university. Usually, transport is erratic in villages as many people drive and the rest are most likely retired. So, we made an offer on both houses, which we eventually didn't get.

Someone had made an offer above the asking price on the expensive house, whilst the other house owner accepted a cash offer. It was disheartening as we had raised our expectations that we would be moving into a village. We have learnt that you can be financially ready and in an excellent position to buy in every way, but things do not always go in your favour. A farmer may have made every effort to plant good seeds on time, taken time to tend the crops and feed them, yet when harvest time comes, he gets nothing. Not every season is the same; however, one thing we must not forget is that every winter prepares us for a summer.

By the time we got to August 2020, we were getting tired of looking and waiting. One afternoon an estate agent released a new property on the market, which we found ideal. We went to view it and fell in love straight away. As with the first property, the house was on sale due to a divorce. We prayed for redirection. This time we were aware of how to handle the process. We made an offer, and the sellers asked us to revise it. Although we had not learned any tips on making offers, we asked the estate agent how many others were interested. They told us one other couple had put an offer slightly above ours. The owner asked us to revise our offer first and give the best price before giving a second refusal to the next person.

The house had been on the market for less than a week. We were aware the area was desirable, and the last house sold on the street had been three years ago. We felt that God was telling us that we had found the right house. We realised that if we didn't make an offer straight away, someone else would outbid us. From our previous experience searching and viewing houses, we knew that multiple buyers would be interested in a house in such a desirable area. As expected, the property didn't stay long on the market. Due to the changes made by the government concerning stamp duty, many people were willing to pay more for properties.

The sellers accepted our offer, and we wanted to move in straight away and asked them to take it off the market. But unfortunately, we couldn't engage a different conveyancer as we would have to pay the old one a full fee. As a result, we raised some issues with them and requested they speed up the process considering our circumstances.

I believe that with God, all things are possible. We didn't face any issues or delays whatsoever this time around. Everyone concerned handled the transaction swiftly and smoothly, and the sellers were very cooperative. We communicated outside of the estate agency and checked up on the progress every weekend. We felt at peace with our relationship with the sellers; we discussed all issues openly between ourselves.

We finally moved into our dream home the first week of November 2020. What a year and a half of waiting and believing.

Takeaway Nuggets

1. Know what you want and be clear about it.
2. Consider all options available and seek help where possible.
3. Prepare yourself for any purchase and have a checklist.
4. Never go for what you can't afford.
5. Always have an open mind, do not limit yourself.
6. Think of plan B when things don't seem to work.
7. Never settle for less.

Chapter 4

Unforeseen Challenges

The terror of the unforeseen is what the science of history
hides, turning a disaster into epic.

PHILLIP ROTH

Farmers have to deal with the many unforeseen challenges that come with each season. During the planting and rainy season, weeds spring up to attack and disrupt the crops that are struggling to come up. Some seasons encounter a drought, destroying whatever harvest the farmers have been anticipating. Then there is always the pests and wild animals that also attack the crops while they are growing. These are challenges that farmers encounter in the process of cultivating their crops. Nevertheless, farmers don't give up because of a challenging season; they face the obstacles head-on, fighting to realise their bumper harvest.

Buying a house can be a complicated and scary undertaking; the finances and emotions involved create a huge cocktail of stress. However, one thing that kept us focused was the need to remain committed. My teacher in high school taught us that commitment is proved by the actions we take while going through adversity. Being able to handle challenges is what makes us triumph.

Investors face risks and challenges daily; they may be affected by a sudden fall in interest rates or a credit crunch, taking all their savings and leaving them with nothing. They are affected by Taxes, politics, recessions, and anything that can happen anytime. They can wake up to finding that these unsteady variables in the market have wiped out all the savings they had invested. Seasoned investors do not give up; they study and watch the market, making strategic moves to protect their investments.

Similarly, Christians encounter testing times in their walk with God. Experience has shown that the devil attacks the most when something great is about to occur. Having a strong faith and reading the Word of God is the most potent weapon we can use to fight Satan's traps. Through our house moving season, we decided not to look at our limiting factors. The COVID-19 situation came as another challenge in our season when we were already facing other challenges.

The going can be tough

When the World Health Organisation announced the discovery of the COVID 19 virus, we had no idea it would become a global pandemic. We thought it was a Chinese problem and so were utterly shocked when the UK government declared a national lockdown in March 2020 to control the spread of the virus. The pandemic changed our plans as many issues affecting home buyers surfaced:

- The housing market closed, conveyances, estate agents' offices, including all stakeholders involved in the property-related business, ceased to operate. As a result, our house buying project came to a halt, and we had to put all other plans aside.

- Even the search queries we had raised stopped, and we were left hanging, not knowing how to proceed.

- Our conveyancers did not inform us about the closures, even though we knew some were working from home. It became clear that all timescales for the exchange of contracts would not be met.

- We had no idea when the government would lift the Lockdown; it was frightening not knowing what would happen with the purchase of our home.

- Finally, the lockdown made it impossible for us to know how committed the sellers and professionals involved were to meet the timescales.

It was challenging to plan our next move as more bad news kept coming our way. The closing of businesses meant that some people were made redundant while others got furloughed. We were not informed of any of these developments by our conveyancers. The conveyancer representing our purchase was furloughed; no one informed us. The whole process suffered delays as there was no one to pick up calls, handle queries or process our paperwork at the company. We experienced a mixture of confusion and fear of the unknown as we had no idea of the progress of our case. We were left hanging, unable to communicate with either the conveyancers or the estate agents for a while.

The obstacles were such that it would have been easier to give up, but we recalled the words of our financial advisor, who'd advised that we should always allow our vision to inspire us to keep a confident attitude. Success calls for patience, hard work and focus on the end goal.

Critical workers within the essential services kept working long hours, dealing with emergencies. Richard was one of those who stayed away, working continuously, which affected our plans. We could not sit down as a family to discuss our situation and the way forward. No one knew how long we would be in lockdown. I held on to the Word from Isaiah 41:10, "Do not fear, for I am with you; do not be discouraged, for I am your God. I will strengthen you; I will uphold you with my righteous hand." Knowing that I had someone watching over me comforted and gave me strength.

When we initially moved in with our friends, we did not expect to stay for more than a couple of weeks; the accommodation offered was not guaranteed forever. However, once businesses shut, it became difficult to find alternative accommodation, even short-term rentals. Furthermore, no house viewings were allowed, and new tenants could not be processed even where the parties involved agreed before the pandemic. The delays meant that we couldn't move out of our friend's house until the government eased the lockdown restrictions.

There was nowhere to go; this was a situation no one could have foreseen. It was not ideal, considering we had initially promised our friends that our situation would be resolved in no time. Instead, the lockdown lasted for over three months, bringing about more uncertainties, confusion and fear. We were stuck, not knowing how to proceed with the property. Should we give it up or hold on until after the lockdown? The thing that reassured us was the knowledge that other buyers were in a similar situation as us. It was a bit encouraging, and it brought some form of comfort to us.

Going through difficult times requires us to run towards them instead of shying away. COVID- 19 invaded our world in a way that no one could have foreseen. Its impact was sharp and deadly. Some people were sick; others suffered different kinds of loss, changing their lives forever. Not having a home of our own during that time wasn't the best experience; our endurance was tested, waking up each day not knowing what lay ahead. We recognised that we had to face considerable costs in storage charges, transport and increased household bills.

There were food shortages; certain foods were missing on supermarket shelves, which required us to go shopping more often than usual to stock up. It became hard to find foods like eggs, flour, toilet paper and soap. Even if one had money, there was nowhere to get food, and many had to reduce daily meals from the required three. Dealing with the food shortages and the raging pandemic and Lockdown was stressful for many families, impacting people's mental health and causing low self-esteem and nutrient deficiencies. As a family, we may never understand how we survived through it all, but what we do know is that we were there for each other. We always discussed our thoughts and sharing our feelings.

It was not always possible for us to visit the supermarket every day whilst staying with other people. It was best to go very early in the day if we were to get the essentials when we did. Going out was risking everyone's health as it meant waiting for hours in queues, being exposed to the other shoppers. There was never a guarantee that we would get all the groceries we needed, so the cycle would repeat itself and went on for weeks as people were panic buying. It became difficult to maintain our usual diet, and we adjusted to eating what was available. It was of utmost importance that we ensure that everyone in our household was kept safe.

Remain grateful

It is not unusual for one season to have both winter and summer experiences. We can never go wrong by giving thanks, proclaiming, or acknowledging even the most minor of things. The COVID period was characterised by some food price hikes, mainly for much-sought-after products like antibacterial soap, flour, and toilet roll. In addition, the government introduced guidelines, including social distancing of 2 metres apart for everyone's safety. There were constant reminders about the regular washing of hands using soap or antibacterial wash.

It became unsafe for two families with children to live together. We had to practice social distancing, which was not easy as some family members worked as keyworkers. Having a combination of people who go to work and children going into university brought many anxieties. It became difficult to talk within someone else's space. It was increasingly alarming if somebody sneezed or coughed because it was automatically associated with COVID-19. At the same time, we could not hug or kiss, neither could we share food or drinks. The stress levels for many was high. Everything that was once normal was now increasingly uncomfortable and distressing. It was a blessing that we didn't have vulnerable individuals or anyone from the high-risk category in the house; we thanked God for this blessing during our prayers.

People were dying at home and in the hospitals. Each day we waited to hear the government updates on the Covid situation, but we could not even watch the TV together in the same room. It was frightening to think what would happen if one of us caught COVID-19, got sick, or died. We remained fearful that things could get worse anytime or that any one of us could be affected. It was nerve-wracking to think of it, considering that we had nowhere to go, so we made sure to look after ourselves well. Regardless of our position, we needed to adapt to the new rules and guidance which the government unveiled daily through their updates. As we adapted, we had to trust God that we were on the right course with Him by our side guiding us. Day by day, we needed to pray and increase our faith in His ability to protect us. Finally, we offered gratitude for life, love and peace during that time. In addition, each day, we prayed for those affected by this awful COVID situation and gave thanks for the blessing we had.

Sometimes life will surprise us. It doesn't matter how much we plan and prepare for every possible outcome; sometimes, things will still go wrong. However, this does not mean that when our expectations face certain risks, we should doubt God. Our Creator knows when every plan will come to pass; regardless, the Lord always orders man's steps (Proverbs 20:24). Even though we may have our plans, Yahweh directs them; He is the one who chooses the best for us. Who knew that the pandemic would disrupt our plans? We were homeless; sometimes, we need to accept a situation that has got out of our control. To accept the situation is to surrender it before the maker, that we may receive His grace. We may not be able to change the situation; however, we can adapt to it.

There was much suffering around, and with this in mind, we understood that our situation was not by accident; God had a plan, even though we were not aware of it. Similarly, anger, disappointment or failure can be parts of life, but we should never let them become our default emotions. Instead, our choice to live from a place of gratitude brings peace.

Being presented with unexpected challenges when we were expecting progress and victory was agonising. As I reflect on the story of Job from the Bible, I realised what happened to him was not his fault. It was a mere response to his integrity and achievements. Job went through a phase where he lost everything he had acquired in a split second. These are some of the agonising experiences that a life season can bring. Not only did he lose his wealth but his children and health. Yet he endured all this and still blessed the name of the Lord. I was convinced that what we were going through was just a test that we could win. God has made us all winners in every life challenge. The bible speaks of us as overcomers in every life challenge (Romans 8:37). What we needed was the time and chance within that time to win, and we can win by acknowledging or saying a simple "thank you" to those who came through for us.

We found it reassuring to remember that "everything had happened for a reason", even as Job's outlook changed for the better. We often prayed to ask the Lord to give us the grace to know why we were in this predicament. Yet the Bible also reminds us to be thankful in all circumstances, for it is the will of God for us who belong to Christ Jesus (I Thessalonians 5:18). To give thanks is to accept that the situation will change us somehow for the better. As we do so, we expect that out of the situation, something good will come. As difficult as it was in our case, we had to learn to say thank you, Lord, each day through prayers.

Keep learning; there's always a lesson

Our lives often bring ongoing learning experiences. Some life lessons are only experienced when we face particular situations. However, some of the lessons may come too late, finding us unprepared. Suffice it to say, we took something away from each lockdown imposed by the government. We realised the need to be deeply rooted in Christ Jesus by reading the Word and praying. As we dug deeper into the Word, it brought a solid understanding of God's purpose in our lives and especially in what was happening during that season. It was not a time to pray for the usual; the focus was more specific on what God said regarding pandemic situations. We must stand in the knowledge that the Creator knows our needs. Jehovah provided us with healing and peace amid the pandemic and the housing predicament. Initially, we wondered how it would work out since we didn't have our own home. However, staying at home in quarantine was a blessing even though we were not in our comfort zone; we had the time to read the Word of God and to pursue other activities of interest. The situation we found ourselves in propelled us into our best lives and allowed us to connect with our Creator effectively.

During that time of isolation, we drew closer to God by the power of the Holy Spirit. Building oneself spiritually helps fight the devil's plans, the enemy of our destiny. We often waste time chasing events that do not add value to our lives. Taking time to pause and think through was refreshing; we started thinking the right thoughts and exercising healthy mindsets. Focusing our thoughts on the pandemic was unhelpful. With that in mind, we chose to walk our journey more positively. We also changed meal plans and food choices and started eating healthy to nurture a balanced immune system and a healthy body. It is from practising such that we appreciated our health which we needed to endure our tribulations. More so, it became one way of developing healthy habits early on to prevent eventual problems.

We were inspired by the old Roman proverb, *"seize the day."* It spoke clearly to us that we should not hesitate where there was a need to act. Failure to act displays a lack of confidence. By taking charge of our day, we would be aware of what was happening in our lives.

I began journaling meal plans to buy food in bulk ahead of cooking because we could not visit the supermarket every day. Staying in the house meant that I could work out the foodstuff available and weigh if it would be enough for our meals. As a result, we noticed that we could save a lot of money by planning, something we had not done before as a family. As a result, our groceries' bill improved slowly; we don't have to buy unnecessary things.

The COVID-19 pandemic taught us to prioritise our lives. Life goes faster than we can imagine; it is not guaranteed and is short-lived. It is, therefore, one's duty to make every moment count. It was humbling to realise that to be alive was a blessing; life is fragile. So, we stopped murmuring and complaining and started looking for the good around us, things to go after and explore.

I considered the sort of legacy I could leave behind for my children and family. We agreed that we needed to start acquiring knowledge to do certain things like small projects to help improve our finances. It was then that I started writing this book; I found it therapeutic to both the mind and body. We made time to share our plans and dreams; I taught my daughter how to knit, something I had not thought about, which strengthened our bond. We also learnt to paint and decorate in preparation for the new house, and my husband learnt to cook African meals. We recognised that we could be flexible with our goals.

The COVID-19 pandemic brought great opportunities for helping those in need. The famous Bible story about the good Samaritan reminded us about the need to be there for the more vulnerable people around us. I began helping those in need by doing grocery shopping for them. As a family, we agreed to share half of our groceries with others each week. I felt so optimistic about doing the things I enjoy most. In our church, I coordinate an African women's prayer group to support and empower one another through different activities. I started collecting a list of people who needed help and made sure I dropped a cooked meal and some specific items for them. I came together with friends, and we collected money and bought food parcels for a few families in the community.

I met daily on Zoom with a group of women intercessors for prayer. We shared updates on the pandemic situation, and there were opportunities for feedback and sharing of experiences. This was an encouragement to others, especially those affected by the pandemic, in one way or another. When we could not meet on Zoom, there was an opportunity to speak to people over the phone to get their specific concerns and pray for them.

Mental health issues were on the rise during the lockdown. Many people we spoke to were exposed to issues like depression, anxiety, suicide, and starvation. The situation was made worse by the lack of sunshine and fresh air as we spent most of the time indoors. I often felt some mental strain and depression because of the situation we found ourselves in. Despite having food in the house, I had no appetite, no desire to eat. We all responded differently to what was happening, we can all be in the same storm, but our boats may not fare the same. I was aware that my anxieties, loneliness, and hopelessness about the situation might have triggered my response to it.

We did our best and learnt to manage the situation by:

- Drinking lots of water
- Playing indoor games
- Meditation and prayer
- Talking about our situation and accepting it
- Taking long walks daily
- Listening to encouraging music

In the Bible, Ezekiel was shown dry bones in a vision. God instructed him to prophesy life to the dead bones (Ezekiel 37). Our situation had become as dry as the dry bones in the Bible story; therefore, I held them in prayer and affirmed a resurrection of life to the situation we found ourselves in. Sometimes we have to approach our life seasons this way.

Money, vision, self-respect are pillars that hold up the health of a family. We may not have been sick physically, but we were feeling the effects of it. We were impacted mentally and emotionally. Our family had been in isolation, and initially, we felt we had missed out on many blessings. Regardless, one cannot take back the joys of the quality time we shared, including that we survived.

Takeaway Nuggets

1. We can all leave a legacy for our family; what will be yours?
2. Look after your mental well-being when going through challenges.
3. Be grateful even for the smallest things around you.
4. Life is worth living; make every moment count.
5. Live fully and learn continually.
6. Be patient and never lose focus of your goal.
7. Surrender your worries and challenges to the creator who knows it all.

Chapter 5

Due Diligence

Buying a home today is a complex process, but that in no way excuses home buyers from their obligation for due diligence.

HENRY PAULSON

Buying a family home is a significant investment and should be an exciting experience. However, sometimes things do not always go according to plan; therefore, one should carefully analyse the risks and uncertainties involved in property purchases. There is also a need to ensure that full house inspections are completed; This is the necessary due diligence. Benjamin Franklin once said, *"diligence is the mother of good luck."* Whatever we set our hearts to do, we must learn to exercise due diligence from the start; when we do so, success is sure to follow.

The Cambridge dictionary defines due diligence as, *"the steps considered reasonable for people to take in order to keep themselves or others in their property safe."*

However, in Real Estate, due diligence is defined *as an investigation of diverse facets of the property carried by a buyer either before making an offer or before signing contracts, (Boccadutri, 2017).*

The expectation is that where any faults are discovered on a property, they should be included within the contracts. This is only if the buyer is happy to continue with the purchase; otherwise, they can pull out. Carrying the necessary feasibility study helps develop an appropriate way forward; it is essential to consider doing anything connected with house purchasing.

Confucius, a Chinese Philosopher, said that *"the expectations of life depend upon diligence; a mechanic that would perfect his work must sharpen his tools."* When exercising one's due diligence during house buying, one must consider every aspect at each stage, weighing the pros and cons then summing up the expectations. This responsibility lies with the buyer.

Similarly, when farmers are approaching a new season, they make sure all the necessary preparations are completed in advance. The Bible states that *"good planning and hard work lead to prosperity, but hasty shortcuts lead to poverty." (Proverbs 21:5, NIV).* There is a warning there about the dangers of poor planning. Nobody would want to make errors when buying a house, especially those that can be easily avoided. Making errors can be costly. Taking time to investigate and analyse everything about the sale is recommended to make better decisions in the buying process. There are various steps involved when buying a house; likewise, there are also actions that a buyer can take to ensure the purchase does not become a nightmare.

Due diligence in buying a property involves:

*   Getting to know the area.
*   Carrying full inspections.
*   Surveying.
*   Checking insurances to dealing with appraisals and restrictions.
*   Checking any outstanding debt against the property.

When one has done their homework carefully and managed to get all the details upfront, there is a confidence that everything will work out well. In addition, getting all the relevant information ahead of the transaction contributes to speeding up the purchase time. When all possible information relating to the property has been brought together and checked, the outcome will inform the buyer of the following action to take.

Instruct qualified and experienced professionals

Most of the work involved in house buying requires enlisting the knowledge and expertise of some professionals. In their capability, buyers are not qualified to carry out searches. They need to know about the design and understand contracts of sale and other documentation. Homebuyers should consider engaging the services of qualified professionals to achieve a smooth process. We carried out some preliminary work regarding the house we wanted to buy as part of due diligence. As a family, we discussed the procedure for successful purchasing and hoped to obtain all the information we needed about the house when the seller accepted our offer. Our responsibility was to carry the necessary investigation on the property with the help of the conveyancers and the seller's solicitors. We soon discovered that we did not seem to have been clear about their role; we misunderstood the role of a conveyancer.

A conveyancer is usually a professional individual or solicitor who assists the buyer with the settlement and title transfer. They ensure that their clients meet all legal obligations and that their client's rights are protected during a purchase. It is recommended that both the buyer and seller engage a conveyancing professional's services as they will have specific obligations to fulfil within a contract of sale. In addition, using a conveyancer or conveyancing solicitor helps in keeping the process streamlined. Some of the primary duties of a conveyancer include:

- Preparing contracts of sale.
- Conducting title and planning searches.
- Prepare transfer documents.
- Legal advice.
- Statutory fees information.
- Organising settlement.

(GAILLAUMES, 2020)

42

When buying a house, one must entrust the support of a licenced conveyancer or solicitor. In the case of a solicitor, they must be a fully qualified lawyer who has received legal training necessary to help give clients advice regarding mortgage documents or other services. A licenced conveyancer has a speciality in property services only; therefore, he will not offer some advice should a client require some legal support. Conveyancers are usually equipped to carry out property sales quickly. However, they are less likely to advise property disputes if a purchase doesn't go well. Regardless, a buyer's legal conveyancers must provide detailed information about the house, including other details that cannot be found during viewings or surveys (*Zoopla,2021*).

When one goes through a winter season, they must be ruled by the head, not their heart. The same applies to engaging a conveyancer; the buyer expects them to be honest and transparent in their dealings. More importantly, they need to provide feedback to the buyer consistently. It is part of good ethics in work and their due diligence. We discovered that sometimes standard due diligence might not be enough, especially when selling a house involving a divorce. There will be a need to engage additional services like a full surveyor's report. Everything must be clear from the onset, and the conveyancer should help the buyer gather all information. We realised the conveyancer we chose was not working alone on the case, they worked with a team, but we did not know whether each member was a trained conveyancer.

The conveyancers that were dealing with our purchase charged for representing us and carrying all the necessary checks. We did not check their reviews immediately or compare their quotes with other firms. It does not matter whether you know the company; checking their reviews will reveal whether they offer a good service. We did not know whether we got a fair price on their quote; neither did we know what services were included. However, the searches carried out were basic and did not unearth any problems. The only issues raised were some cosmetic redecoration jobs, carpets and servicing the boiler. With this information, we felt everything would be straightforward from then onset. Little did we know we were supposed to keep checking every detail and raising queries promptly. We did not know whether the searches were enough to complete both the legal and financial processes. Our ignorance in these matters was to be our downfall in this house-buying season.

Take responsibility

During summer seasons, farmers sometimes face a battle to fight pests that come to eat their crops. In our case, the need to carry out some redecorating work or install a new boiler would be part of fighting in the battleground. Consequently, there will be times like these when we face one trial after another in our Christian walk. If one chooses to give up, they will not harvest. Sydney Smith said, *"a great deal of talent is lost to the world for want of little courage."* Timidity should never push us to the grave. Therefore, we must fight and believe in God for a bumper harvest. It can be frustrating to be in such a situation, but we must always understand God's will for us in every season. Once we understand, it doesn't matter how many winters we have gone through; we will continue to hold on to what we believe.

The searches produced by the conveyancers did not include a full report from a certified home inspector or surveyor. We did not choose to explore this because the house looked good. Carrying out a complete home inspection does not come cheap. We thought it would be an unnecessary spend as the house was not old and looked perfect for us. We naively thought we were fortunate that only the boiler needed a report since its last service. Our conveyancers did not advise the need for a home inspector.

We were taken aback when it became apparent that there was no guaranteed completion in good time; we didn't do anything other than wait and gave everything to the Lord in prayer. We prayed for the conveyancers and estate agents. It seemed as if we had forgotten that faith without action is dead (James 2:26). Since we could not speak to any of the professionals, we decided to pray for them instead, even when it was hard to accept the situation. Praying strengthened our resolve to continue pursuing the process and doing anything we could think of that would help. Unfortunately, mistakes do happen because of human error, and it became difficult to trust the professionals. Our faith was truly tested, but we stood firm in prayer.

There was no chain process attached to our house purchase, yet the professionals did not provide any proposals regarding completion. Going by basic calculations, completing the process should have been at the beginning of February. We didn't raise any concerns about this as we should have; the pandemic complicated everything. Furthermore, there was no plan on how the conveyancer intended to move things along. Our failure to query things cost us in that respect; we could have demanded to know every step ahead. There were more challenges to come.

When we became aware of the selling couple's divorce, we hoped everything else would be clarified within reason. Unfortunately, the sellers' estate agent told us different things, and our conveyancer did not help us with our enquiries. Once we insisted on getting more information, we felt that their solicitors were avoiding our calls. It seemed the estate agent had no strategy in place for the move from office to home working. The problem worsened because they were not taking our calls and only accepting emails, which is not the best way to deal with house purchases. Even though we understood the communication breakdown was due to the COVID-19 pandemic, it became difficult to believe anyone.

It became clear that the sellers had been struggling to reach an agreement regarding the debts attached to the house. We approached the estate agent seeking clarification and learned the house had to be sold. However, issues around confidentiality did not allow them to talk about anything else but the house. There was no collaboration between the professionals, and the information available was limited. We had no idea what was happening.

It never occurred to us that we needed someone else to advise us about the steps to take; we felt let down by our conveyancers who were not working for us, neither did they seem to have our best interests at heart. As a result, we waited, expecting things to turn around for the better. It became clear that the house buying process is sometimes dependant on professionals pushing their paperwork and communicating between themselves and us. None of this was happening. Once the searches revealed some restrictions on the house, we expected to get more information on moving forward. Unfortunately, we had not met the sellers before, so we could not contact them directly for further information. Although their divorce was none of our business, we felt it could have been better if we had received some clarity from "the horse's mouth."

With due diligence comes one's moral responsibility. As much as we expected the conveyancers to do much of the work, our ignorance of specific information was no excuse. Abhijit Naskar once said, *"knowing what is moral is easy, acting on it is the difficult part."* To succeed in our endeavours, we must take specific steps in breaking the inertia that holds us back. Success will be difficult to achieve if we do not challenge some of the limitations that hold us back.

We soon learnt that our lead solicitor had been furloughed and left junior conveyancers to deal with our case. We assumed they knew their job; however, it became clear they had put our file aside and never made any appropriate follow up on it. We were disappointed and discouraged, but we could not fire them as we would incur some costs for the work already done. Considering the time that had lapsed, we thought the charges would be too high, and we didn't want to end up in debt, so we kept them. Soon our case became even more complicated as more debts were unveiled on the house. Our conveyancers told us that we had to wait, and no further explanation was offered on how complex the process had become. We believed this would be their duty of care to a customer. Instead, they kept telling us that we should not worry because the problem would be resolved quickly.

Act decisively

In Psalms 118:24, We are reminded about the newness of each day, but also that today is different from yesterday, "this is the day the Lord has made; let us rejoice and be glad in it." (NIV). Therefore, we must get up and take charge of what is given to us each day. Lailah Gifty Akita encourages us to seek the blessings each day brings. We can do this by reflecting on yesterday and finding what we can do differently today. We can then act and create a to-do list for the day based on what we can see and what needs doing; there should be no complacency. Our failure to do something will only hinder us from seeing the blessings released for us. With a to-do list, we can seek to accomplish one thing each day. Then, as we start to reset our goals, we can feel more empowered, and our minds are free to explore possibilities.

We learnt that with a to-do list, we could manage one's time and act diligently. In addition, having a to-do list reduces the stress and anxiety of not knowing what to do. Similarly, a to-do list helps with checks and balances, ensuring that you are in the driving seat as a buyer rather than reacting when encountering a problem. For example, we later found out that we could have bought a little book to list every task that needed completing at each stage of the buying process.

Hindsight is amazing

As time went on, we realised we had never bothered to check how long the house had been vacant. On speaking to some neighbours on the street, we discovered the house had been empty for almost two years. This fact was just one of the clues that something was wrong from the start. Looking back at the process, we thought it could have helped if we'd had more information about the divorce. We should have scrutinised the seller or got more information through our conveyancers to help us make more practical and informed decisions.

On the other hand, we were trying to remain in a place of compassion and trust. Unfortunately, our case proved more and more complicated as time went on.

The complications attached to our house required a property expert or solicitor; we felt that our conveyancers were not displaying their expertise on the case, which further complicated the situation. Sometimes it is expected that the estate agent should share any material earlier on at the viewing stage. In our case, nothing was shared. Neither did we receive further updates and clarifications on the house debts. We felt that it was necessary to know how soon the issues would be resolved to consider our options accordingly.

We should have been concerned that we could not locate the sellers, and this is very unusual as in many cases, buyers can meet the sellers unless they live out of town or abroad. Seeking advice from a solicitor would have assisted us regarding when to pull out from the sale. It became clear that conveyancers are sometimes more concerned about getting their money than what they can do for the customer. As a result, we started losing confidence in the process. I often became anxious about what was coming next. Little did we know that we could have stepped things up by carrying out our inspections independently and pushing to get information quickly. The word of God teaches us to hold on to Him during demanding projects like house buying. It was a time to get close to God in prayer for answers and guidance.

The process taught us that we must take responsibility and follow up at every stage instead of expecting someone else to do it for us. We could have done this through prompting or chasing up daily whilst demanding answers. This would have enabled us to develop a sound strategy about when to exit from the offer. It took us a long time to decide that we no longer wanted to proceed, but the damage had already been done. Unfortunately, we had not prepared our minds to handle that.

In the world we live in, there is so much hostility. The word of God encourages us, *"Be on the alert, stand firm in the faith, act like men, be strong"* (1 Corinthians 16:13NIV). We need to be aware of who we are dealing with to do our part accordingly. Further, it helps us to have the ability to know where to draw the line or remain hopeful. When He was sending His disciples in Mathew 10:16, Jesus warned them to be wise as serpents. As Jesus' followers, the same applies to us; we needed to do our part and leave the rest for God. We live in a world where people disappoint others by breaking their trust. Yet, in matters of house buying, trust is a must or is assumed to be given.

There is a story in the Bible of a persistent woman who kept coming before a judge seeking justice for her case (Luke 18:1-8). The judge had to resolve this matter because of the woman's persistence, and eventually, the case was resolved in the woman's favour. Our house-buying ordeal is an example where we needed to persist with different questions at every stage. When we realised that the conveyancers did not seem to be doing their work, we needed to step up and pursue them with either a visit to their offices or phone calls. If they'd had someone persistently on their back, it might have made them work on our case more diligently.

It was not a good practice that the delays in the process resulted from a lack of information sharing not appropriately handled by the professionals handling our case. The fact that some critical information regarding the debts was not disclosed appropriately by the professionals proved to be dishonesty on the seller's side. We realised that sometimes it is crucial to seek an explanation for delays in releasing documentation. All we kept receiving were the uncertainties surrounding the completion of the purchase. We felt like we were part of the divorce proceedings going on between the sellers. Our move depended on the sellers and their estate agents whilst they appeared to have offloaded their case for somebody else to deal with. Sometimes God can use a time of confusion between professionals and their customers to show that He is in control. Eventually, Yahweh will do it His way. I felt that it didn't matter how much we investigate, plan, and structure; the overall instruction would come from God. As such, we must decide to live life to the full, making the most of every opportunity within any given situation.

We began to wonder if we had made a mistake by using the conveyancers or choosing that house. Our daughter suggested holding the conveyancer responsible without fear of being called problematic people. Perhaps we should have paid more by hiring a property specialist to take this on. However, it didn't seem like good timing, although it could have helped minimise the risk. There were some great reviews for the conveyancer on paper, but that wasn't the case. This was a valuable teaching point for us to be vigilant in making decisions. In future, we know carrying out solid due diligence minimises risks and stress. If they didn't deliver, then one could drop them straightaway and engage someone else. We can stay on top of progress as there is a good chance of understanding what's going on. Where due diligence has taken place, we are prepared for any delays. Without due diligence, the process of house buying can be frustrating instead of being enjoyed.

Takeaway Nuggets

1. Be sure you understand every aspect of your purchase.

2. Go for the right professionals and understand how they work.

3. Always compare quotes of services.

4. Take personal responsibility and act.

5. Plan your actions and do a daily checklist.

6. Never procrastinate on things; understand your role from the beginning.

7. Do not be afraid of raising queries or holding professionals responsible.

Chapter 6

Stepping out of the Comfort Zone

Your comfort zone is your weak zone. Get up and move.
                                            OLAWALE DANIEL

"*Coming out of your comfort zone is tough in the beginning, chaotic in the middle and awesome in the end... because in the end, it showed you a whole new world.*" (Manoj Arora). We have the power to move out of our comfort zone. It is a personal decision that one makes; however, taking that bold step requires discipline. In as much as it's not easy, we know that life will not remain the same. It's so much easier to stay in one's comfort zone because stepping out is challenging and filled with many "unknowns." To take that bold stride requires a certain degree of faith. However, in life, we may sometimes find ourselves in circumstances that push us into seizing the moment and doing things we've never done. These may be undertakings that appeared difficult before or that we never thought we could do.

Fear is usually one of the major stumbling blocks to taking action. Many people are afraid of what will happen if they fail. The thought of previous failures may be one of our limiting beliefs to living successfully. Regardless, we must not forget that staying in our comfort zone is a trap. The Bible in 2 Timothy 1:7 reminds us that *God did not give us a spirit of fear but one that is of power, love and self-discipline.* (NIV).

In his article, "Start Here", Joseph Mavericks encourages commitment and repetition for people to succeed. The Bible also rightly tells us that *God did not give us a spirit of fear* (2 Timothy 1:7). To move from the comfort zone, one must love change and adopt self-discipline. As we walked our house buying journey through, we realised from our predicament that we had some steps to take and tasks to complete. We needed to make daily commitments and adopt self-discipline.

Our comfort zone contains what we have, family, friends, money, health, jobs and home. Whatever things we desire and do not have is found outside the comfort zone. We, therefore, have to leave our comfort zone or do something different to attain the things we desire. The way our house buying situation unravelled caught us off guard and, after that, we were forced to go with whatever option was available. I am now constantly reminded of the need to pray for the grace to endure each moment without regrets. All the same, I know that the Lord will always protect and uphold us in whatever process we go through. Deuteronomy 31:8 says that "it *is the Lord who goes before us; He will be with us.*" (NIV). We must, therefore, not be afraid or dismayed in any circumstance.

Things changed once we turned up at our friends' place. Our lives were packed in our boxes. We were a little apprehensive at being in someone else's home; we did not know what to expect. Richard had never lived in someone else's house before; His experience was limited to visiting others for a few hours and returning to his home. Coming from Africa, where families live together for long periods of time, living with others was nothing new for my daughter and me. It was not the first time we lived with others in the UK as previously we had lived with cousins and friends. When I first arrived in the UK, I stayed with a friend's family for over six months while settling and eventually finding my place. I took our present circumstances as an opportunity to reflect upon my personal growth and skills gained over the years. We all need to keep developing our communication, interacting, listening and relationship skills.

Adapt to the situation

Being in someone else's home meant that we had to be on our best behaviour and respect their space. My husband constantly reminded us to keep things simple and remember that we were not in our own home, but guests in someone's home. We remained grateful every day, remembering that it was a privilege to have friends who could accommodate us in times of crisis.

Before moving in with our friends, I offered to lead worship, prayer and share the word with an interdenominational women's group that I was a part of. Consequently, the group tasked me to teach every Monday morning, which I fulfilled from January without any problems, finding it enjoyable. However, when we moved, it became challenging to deliver any prayers on the phone without disrupting the routine of the home we were now living in. In addition, I had to be mindful of others during prayers and Bible study times. Being mindful of others helps in building stronger relationships and makes us better people. Such simple considerations bring peace and joy to all around.

When we were in our home, I used my study room for Bible study and prayers. Things had changed, and I was pleading with God from a different environment for the time being. It wasn't that there was no space; I was using the bedroom where we slept, and it wasn't the best place to be, especially when Richard had a lay-in. It meant disturbing Richard's sleep, and the same applied to everyone in the house. I felt the urgency for a breakthrough with our house as I realised this was unfair to those around me. Reading the Bible or praying with others on the prayer line demanded that I speak up repeatedly as I wanted the others on the line to hear me. At times I would sing a short song or agree loudly with someone praying. People in the next room would be disturbed by my loud voice. Although no one complained, I realised that I could not continue leading the prayers for the time being. It was unfair on others, so I contacted the group leaders, asking them to find a replacement until I settled in my own home. Immediately my prayer routine and that of my family was out of place, but I still offered gratitude for the experience and the lessons from it.

For a few years, I coordinated a small group of African women from our church voluntarily. Due to the lockdown, we couldn't meet for our usual prayer gatherings; therefore, we started having daily morning prayers at six in the morning and nine at night on a prayer line. Sometimes the prayers would interfere with what was going on in the house that required my input, and I would have to excuse myself from the prayer line. At times I would swap and do what needed doing first, then attend the prayer line the following day. Nevertheless, I found opportunities to speak to group members during my free time. Taking time to listen to others was a great achievement as I could develop my coaching and mentoring skills.

Moving out of our comfort zone often allows us to take risks, but it brings growth in the process. Whatever we do whilst outside our comfort zone acts as a motivation and promotes self-empowerment.

The idea of getting up early to pray in our friends' homes was not so good, bearing in mind that others were asleep. Had it been in my own house, I knew I would have space outside my main bedroom. Every so often, I felt this was a loss of freedom to do what I enjoyed doing; nevertheless, I learned to adjust. On many occasions, we had to remember to be mindful not to make noise. We were afraid that our noise or the children's might make our hosts uncomfortable, disrupting their peace. We also found out that we could not have the quality time as a couple as we used to do, and we kept encouraging each other that things could change overnight, and we would have our lives back.

We had always prayed together and shared Bible reading every weekend when everyone was not busy, but this had to change. We missed the opportunity to spend time with the children. When the country moved into lockdown, everything changed for the church and its people. There was an alternative to participate in church services via zoom and YouTube, which became the new normal for most people. Since our friends are also Christians, we started having more prayers in the house and sometimes watching the services on zoom together. This brought unity and togetherness among us, and I could see the opportunity to impact others, especially those around us. It helped in accelerating our journey to achieving our goal.

When it came to cooking, sometimes we would be limited to space in the kitchen. We could not all be in the kitchen at the same time to prepare different meals. We had to be flexible and adjust cooking times or, at times, order takeaway. Every household has its eating habits, and our friends' food and meal choices differed from ours. My family has always enjoyed cooking, and we love organic foods, but we ordered fish and chips from our local takeaway on Fridays. We took Friday evening to relax after a working week, and as such, there would be no cooking. We all enjoyed our traditional dinner time on Friday, sharing the fish and chips between us. Our eating habits and traditions had to change due to the lockdown; we learnt to adapt and accept that things had changed for the time being.

Home life, as we knew it, changed in that season. The secret to success lies in having a daily routine. Choosing to do one or two things each day that make you happy can be the starting point. We could not have our usual activities in the house, like playing scrabble every Sunday afternoon, which stopped together with some TV programmes we used to enjoy watching together. Covid-19 prevented us from visiting friends nor having people come to our friends' homes to see us. The children were confined and limited to either their bedrooms or dining room at mealtimes. We kicked our routines out of the window and adjusted to the new way of life presented by the season.

Our birthdays and anniversary fell in April, May, June and August, right in the thick of the first wave of Covid, and we could not celebrate them as we would have wanted to. Notwithstanding all that, we learned that we could do without certain things in life and remained appreciative and hopeful. We don't know how we could have survived without family and friends. Instead of buying gifts for celebrating birthdays, we learnt to cook for others who were too ill from Covid to cook for themselves.

Embrace challenges

The Bible encourages us to stay strong and lean on the word of God. According to 2 Corinthians 4:8-9, *"We are hard-pressed on every side, but not crushed; perplexed, but not in despair; persecuted, but not abandoned; struck down, but not destroyed" (NIV)*. This is encouragement that certain seasons may come to destroy us, but they do not last forever. We will remain standing. We learned to be more patient with people and embrace the season. We should all desire the patience to endure troubles. When we are patient, it doesn't mean that we are constantly right, but we can accommodate other people's needs and choices. A Swahili Proverbs says, "Patience attracts happiness; it brings near that which is far".

In 1 Samuel 1-2, Hannah was married to Elkanah as one of his two wives. She was known to be barren. Her husband's second wife, Peninah, tormented her for being childless. Still, Hannah kept praying and was patient with God despite her painful situation. Even though our situation was not like Hannah's, there were qualities such as humility, endurance and trusting God without any concern or doubt that stood parallel. While experiencing difficulties, we realised that we could embrace trust and hope without being distracted by what others say. As a result, we grew strong in our prayer life and in handling challenging situations.

Coming out of our comfort zone required us to remember that we were in a global pandemic. That awareness helped us open our minds and use the time to eliminate any fears we had. We began testing new ideas by stretching our boundaries and knowing that we were at peace with everyone despite all we were going through felt good. Our family needed joy and love regardless of what we were facing.

Trusting the Lord is a fundamental part of every Christian believer. Being in someone else's house does not mean you cannot trust God there as well. The idea of being exposed to another way of living taught us to have confidence in those people around us. As we did so, we were inspired to make positive decisions concerning our situation. It was up to us to trust the people we were living with and enjoy our stay.

Each time we came together, we reflected on the way each one of us was getting on. Sometimes we had specific positive and negative observations, whilst at other times it was negative. We saw the opportunity for introspection, and we all profited from every evaluation. The introspection helps us to come up with better strategies for what lay ahead. It was then up to each one of us to take the feedback seriously and take appropriate action.

We believed that our relationship with our friends would remain good and be strengthened. Philippians 4:12 states that *"I know how to live on almost nothing or with everything."* I have learned the secret of living in every situation, whether it hurts or blesses, and I know there will always be some inspiration.

Takeaway Nuggets

1. When life pushes you out of your comfort zone, get hold of the moment, time is precious.

2. Turn a deaf ear to your failures, allow the lessons out of them to shape you.

3. Stay committed to your dreams; your life will begin to change.

4. When pressure mounts, prayer and meditation help us to feel good.

5. When life seems too complicated, remember that one minute of patience brings ten years of peace.

6. Gratitude turns our focus to the positive in life.

7. Do something new to appreciate your challenge.

Chapter 7

Faith over fear

"Every tomorrow has two handles. We can take hold of it
with the handle of anxiety or the handle of faith."
Henry Ward Beecher

For the Christian believer, growth comes with having faith and confidence in God. According to Hebrews 11, faith is being sure of the things we have a conviction in and having assurance about the things we cannot see. (NIV). The surety is like the foundation that brings about set goals; it believes in everything about the Lord and what He said in His Word, the Bible. The Bible in Mathew 19:26 states that *"With man this is impossible, but with God all things are possible."(NIV)*. Everything about our personal experiences is feasible when we consider the plans of our Creator. The verse above is recited the world over during life challenges. Many have chanted it during career-related prayers, but mainly, Christians have used it during demanding circumstances as a word of encouragement. Above all, this scripture declares the supremacy of Jehovah and His undeniable influence in our existence.

Fear is a self-imposed prison that will keep you from becoming what God intends for you to be. You must move against it with the weapons of faith and love (Rick Warren). If one can choose to be afraid, nothing can stop one from choosing faith. Bearing this in mind, we can choose faith at the right time.

We believed that God determined our house buying course, but it proved to have levels and stages. This gave us a confirmation that it was a season that comes and would go. The Almighty does not always give us everything in one fall, but He gives us blessings in steps. At every stride, one's belief is a deciding factor on how one will come out. Bearing this in mind, we knew the entire period would be a time of growing our faith.

Consequently, when it comes to life seasons, what we experience in our summer season is not what we experience in our winter months. The Almighty causes each phase to be different, and there will be times when we experience severe hardships as we try to achieve our vision. However, at times when we set out to do something, it materialises without any problems.

In the farming world, some seasons are dry, and some are too cold. We find that some grains require chilled weather whilst others can only thrive within a warm climate, and others grow under strict temperature monitoring. There are times when the breed of the seeds will determine when the farmers sow seeds, yet the crop variety will not matter. When the climate is dry, the prospect of sowing and growing any seed is restricted. Only faith will decide whether one will plant during a warm season; faith will also determine whether one will harvest.

We can still grow with faith, but we need to know what seed to grow. The same applies in fulfilling life goals; one needs the confidence to know which door to knock on. One's strength determines that one will get what one wants when the gate opens. When it comes to house buying, we wish to be assured that nothing will come between the case from the beginning to the end of the process. Nevertheless, things can go wrong, and we end up abandoning the whole project. Once we decided to look for an alternative property, it was not easy to get a suitable property within our budget. Praying each day before going for viewings, we asked God for the grace to carry on. We didn't have any idea or an alternative about what we would do if we didn't get a house or if the lockdown stayed on for a long time.

Having the assurance, we needed was the driving force between searching, choosing and purchasing. It was a great motivation during the waiting period from the sold subject to the contract (STC), to signing the contracts. Without it, we would probably have given up buying, considering the issues that arose during the process. As a result, our house buying season became a painful season that needed us to put our hope and trust in God. For us to give up on this dream would have been devastating as God's children; it would be a sign of fear and failure. In addition, surrendering the idea meant that we had failed to cooperate with our Maker in fulfilling His plan to prosper our family.

Discuss your worries

At one point, we sat down to discuss whether we should carry on looking for a house to buy or get a rented property for a year to give ourselves time to recover. We wanted to escape the trauma and burden of the uncertainty of our situation. Renting a property was not our initial plan. We were tired and felt like giving up; we also noticed that we lacked the motivation to pray. Although we had the assurance from God's word as the driving force between searching, choosing and purchasing, it was difficult to hold on to it. We had tried all we could, and unforeseen factors like the pandemic were now in the picture; we felt we were not getting anywhere. I reached out to the women prayer line group and asked if they could carry us in prayer. The prayer group raised prayers for us immediately and released words of encouragement. We felt reassured that God would come through for us, and we began to feel better. Through the next few weeks, we remained hopeful. We continued to receive prayers in the following days and months.

Faith calls for us to welcome the unacceptable even when we have no control over situations. Embracing the obstacles and choosing to live with them is one thing, whilst deciding to keep going despite the obstacle is another. Even when we discovered no suitable house within the few months of searching and viewing, we chose to keep going. We kept standing during the Coronavirus as we waited for the outcome of our offer. Remaining confident was a sign of hope, whilst giving up meant failure to trust in the Lord.

We needed fuel to keep us going; therefore, we discussed programming our minds and emotions to speak positively about our situation. Positive speaking changes our emotional and physical attitudes; it takes the fear away. We began by making declarations each day. Some of the affirmations we made each morning were:

- Today I choose to be anchored in God in everything I do.

- My faith will empower me; I shall not be afraid.

- I am enough to handle today's challenge.

- No weapon fashioned against me shall prosper.

- Giving up is a failure; carrying on is a success; I choose to be successful.

- I am grateful for each challenge I face; there's a way to come out.

Sometimes conviction comes with pain, anger, and frustration. We can also get frustrated because we are not getting what we want. Initially, we couldn't find the house we wanted, but soon after the offer on Dandy Mill View was accepted, we had to face the agony of waiting. This agony was aggravated by professionals (Solicitors, estate agents and mortgage advisors) who were not working efficiently, making the whole project a stressful experience, but we kept trusting Jehovah. Job remained strong through a painful storm in his life. He accepted everything even as he experienced anguish in his soul. Job prayed and resolved to declare to God that "He can do all things" (Job 42:2 NIV).

Job experienced a time of pain and sorrow, but despite all the trials, he still trusted God; he acknowledged His presence in the situation. Job's story confirmed to us that Yahweh is always by our side as His children. He gives us the power we need to accomplish our life goals regardless of whether we succeed or not. Our Heavenly Father is also with us even in the darkest moments, and so therefore we need to have our confidence rooted in Him. For example, our success in buying a home depended on God's presence within the process and His grace over our family.

"God grant me the serenity to accept the things I cannot change; Courage to change the things I can and wisdom to know the difference."

THE SERENITY PRAYER,
REINHOLD NEIBUHR

To have serenity means to have a calm state of mind. Meditating on these words provided a way of acceptance for us. To accept the situation is a way of surrendering your worries which is another way of coping. The more we know and understand our struggles, the better we figure out how to handle them. Whichever way we choose to manage the challenges, we overcome fear and trust that route.

Remember previous victories

We believed in prayer and prayed during the process, even before starting the search. Beseeching is, with no hesitation, quite stimulating. When we pray, we submit all our concerns, affliction, and problems to Yahweh and set them at His tabernacle. Then, we give thanks and wait for a reply. Jehovah's response to our requests will come in His time, so the period of waiting produces faith. For our family, praying about the house situation was an act of loyalty meant to reaffirm our belief in God, asking Him to take care of us along the process, and bring a beautiful, safe and comfortable house to us. We even recalled previous battles the Lord had fought for us and felt hopeful. Once we believed that Jehovah had provided for us in so many ways before, He had availed the finances; therefore, we knew that providing a house for us was not a problem for Him. When we consider God, we usually ask more from Him because of our relationship with Him. We believed Jehovah would meet all our needs according to His riches in glory (Philippians 4:19).

As we waited on our offer on Dandy Mill View to be accepted, praying was like being on a battlefield. We sometimes don't know what to do when the enemy attacks; however, we must look to Jesus in prayer.

Prayer calms the anxieties and tensions of facing the unknown, taking us into times of refreshment. Some battles require spiritual warfare other than facing the giant. Devotion can provide strength; thus, our duty is to draw strength from God. God reminded us that the battle belonged to Him; all we needed was to stand still (2 Chronicle 20:15). Standing still with prayer takes away the worry, and all we felt was a sense of confidence. When we remain confident, our thoughts fill with great expectations, and we can overcome every negativity.

There is power in pleading; when we start praising, the gates to our desires start to open on their accord. Our ability to accept challenges is aided by meditating on the Word and prayer. For example, when we kept getting negative reports from the Dandy Mill View house sellers, our job was to keep speaking to God, reminiscing about previous successes, and giving thanks. In many of the prayers offered, we needed the help of the Holy Spirit. The Holy Spirit is the engine that will speak on our behalf and teach us what to say. He gives us discernment which sometimes comes through the still small voice or a gentle whisper. As the voice comes to us, it brings an instruction, an answer or an assurance about what we are believing for.

The Bible encourages us to be led by the Holy Spirit in what we do (Romans 8:26-27 NIV). In our case, we needed the Holy Spirit to give us peace and the grace to wait. As we wait, the Holy Spirit keeps us informed and confirms things to us. He will speak and intercede for us with groanings, and He will give us guidance on how to handle the developments, reminding us of God's faithfulness. The Holy Spirit, therefore, works in us to will and to act. In addition, He allows us to remain connected to God. We are capable of bearing fruits of success if we remain connected.

Listen attentively

In 2 Chronicles 20:1-25, King Jehoshaphat of Judah heard that the Ammonites, Moabites and the Meunites had come to war against him.

He was troubled and consulted Jehovah for help. Jehoshaphat brought his people together, and they prayed, asking God to intervene on their behalf. God answered through Jahaziel the Prophet and assured Jehoshaphat that he should not be afraid of the large armies coming against him. Instead, God would fight the battle for him, but Jehoshaphat and his people were to march and meet their enemies, face them, and God would take authority. Jehoshaphat worshipped, praised God and encouraged the people to put their hope in God. As they faced their adversary the following morning, believing in the word from God, remembering how He had provided for them before they praised, sang and thanked God. Without fail, God granted them victory. We learnt that the act of facing the enemy shows courage and removed fear. Many battles have been fought and won when people believed in their capabilities.

Our situation was no different from Jehoshaphat's story. Once we realised the complexities of the circumstances involving the Dandy View Mill house, we knew we had battles to fight. Moreso, when the Coronavirus came, it became one problem after another as agencies involved started closing. We had to understand that we didn't need to put much effort into this project; only God would see us through. Our duty was to pray without ceasing. When my family began to give up, I took responsibility as a mother and encouraged them to wait on God to deliver. It was best to remind them where we come from.

We had to arrest unacceptable news and concentrate on service. We refused to speak anything negative about our situation but started to believe in the truth that we would get a house. One evening we took our gratitude list and took turns to recite each one making sure we each added three to the list to make them ten. We, therefore, had ten things to be grateful for in the season and then relax, waiting for the next step. The truth is what we declared with our mouth. By acceptance, we were able to confess victory every day, pronouncing that, "this is our season, we are expecting God's abundance. God, we are looking forward to your favours; we expect your blessings, grace, prosperity, and everything that comes with blessings." This was an act of speaking into the situation.

We often feel stuck in life, without any alternatives, which sometimes increases our fears, especially when we are trapped in situations, we have no control over. The Bible in Deuteronomy 11:26-28 tells us that God has put before us blessings and curses. We have an option to choose a blessing or a curse. Having options gives us the power to make informed decisions and to take charge of our situation. Whatever option we take, this is what we confess with our mouth. Choosing a blessing will produce fruit, whilst taking a curse yields harmful consequences that cause suffering. With suffering comes poverty which can run from generation to generation. Reciting our gratitude list was a way of choosing blessings. In our case, to choose blessings was choosing that the house purchase will go ahead without fail. We enjoyed affirming grace every day, which I believe is one of the conditions for success.

A time came when the solicitors and estate agents could not do much to solve the situation quickly. They used the pandemic as a scapegoat. That said, our trust remained anchored on the faithfulness of God and His provision. In Ephesians 6:13, Paul reminds us that we must stand firm when we have done everything to fight the battle. We must not fall when difficulties come. The devil uses people as his instruments to shake us up; instead, we should stand firm. Boris Mackey mentioned that sometimes we need self -determination and self-examination for us to manage certain situations. Our pain sometimes brings a positive transformation. As we take the step to examine ourselves, we gain the courage to manage our situation. However, this is often difficult as many people find it hard to take a self-examination.

When it comes to self-examination, the choice lies with each person. To remain standing is to keep praying, with conviction, full of joy and peace, giving room for Yahweh to complete the rest of the work by His spirit. Jehovah works with hope and expectations. In the story of Jehoshaphat above, the Lord encouraged him to stand firm and see the victory. They had a choice whether to ignore the promise or take the instruction not to fight the battle but to stand still and watch the deliverance occur. We chose to do the same, believe that things will happen, do our part, and wait for the process. God can turn things around in a split second when we concentrate on Him. Where there is belief, there will be a relief.

Jehovah is our provider, and He desires us to seek Him first. This command to seek Him first was not easy to understand, especially for Richard, who seemed impatient to wait. But, standing still is part of waiting and giving everything to God. Our faith provided us with the truth that the house will come one day. I shared with my family some of the Bible stories where people had to wait on God as encouragement.

Delay does not mean denial unless it's confirmed. Even where it's confirmed, through faith, we can try other alternatives. Many examples from scripture display difficult circumstances where breakthrough seemed impossible, but they did not give up and neither did they settle for less. Such Bible stories boost our faith in the God who works miracles. Even though we cannot see how our miracle will come, knowing that other people have gone through similar circumstances and received their hearts' desires becomes our drive. When we stand still, we allow the testimonies from others to minister to our challenges and energise our efforts.

Although our position was not like any of the stories, learning about them affirmed that prayer changes our perspective on things. The more we seek and understand Jehovah's will in our situation, the more positive we feel, and God comes through and enables us to achieve our desires.

During the waiting, I came across an article by Seagull titled, *"Your address is not by coincidence."* Reading through the piece was eye-opening as it reflected on what people go through while purchasing a home. It gives an example where someone narrated how they had spent over a year waiting for a house purchase to complete. Someone even gave up on one particular house after such a long time only to start all over again. However, in the end, they purchased something much better than the one they abandoned. These stories reassured me that everything works out well in the end, no matter the circumstances or time it takes. My conviction was that where God guides, He provides. No matter how things look, God is still in control. In our moments of facing confusion and fear, we need to be still. When we take time to think things through and come up with options, we can be assured of success.

When we lead every stride by truth, we are in harmony with the Holy Spirit and become acquainted with the Bible. Reading the Word of God helps us to grow our confidence. Romans 10:17 teaches us that faith comes by hearing the word of God. We lived on the Word during our season, believing the scriptures and holding onto what they said concerning our circumstances. We kept reciting and believing Isaiah 43:19," *God will make a way where there seems to be no way*". We also stood on Romans 8:28," All *things work together for good to all those who love God, and those who are called to His purpose*". These scriptures gave us hope and convinced us that God would help us and give us wisdom and understanding to win our battle. As a result, we became less worried, and our confidence increased.

Get a support system

Sometimes God sends us people to walk through a journey with us which helps boost our confidence. The people we walked with throughout our predicament acted as pillars of encouragement. One of our friends always encouraged us about the need to pray, saying, *"where there is a man to pray, there is God to answer; pray always."* Prayer has the power to bring the desired outcome. Sharing this with my family helped us pray and believe that what we were waiting for would come speedily without fail. We were united in worship such that every one of us was in tune to ask. It was from a genuine heart that anyone of us would start praying for strength at every stage.

Our input is needed along the way, from planning finances, searching, and viewing suitable houses to process information and moving in. We needed the courage to see the project through to the end. Even when the situation was unbearable, what we needed was the strength to keep asking. Prayer helped us to push through and enabled us to remain steady. We believed that God was with us through the trials. With such belief, we remained focused on our request, and we found ourselves worshipping everywhere. Worship transmits the capacity to run without a blackout.

"A real friend is one who walks in when the rest of the world walks out" (Walter Winchell). Amongst the friends we walked with during the season, one of them made it her task to ring every day at 7 am checking on the progress of things and sharing some thoughts on the next step. It reminded me of the story of the paralytic man from the Bible (Mark 2:1-12). The man was brought by his friends on a stretcher to Jesus for healing. His friends brought him because he could not do it himself. When we are weak and helpless, sometimes we need others to carry us through to a place of victory by prayer and support. Our situation felt like that of the paralytic man, but coping was made easier with the help of friends.

Talking about our situation with friends opened an opportunity to share their own experiences of when they went through challenges. Listening and learning from their wisdom was motivating; hearing how they overcame their challenges inspired us. Having friends praying with us and reassuring us was comforting and helped us know that we had a support system. It inspired and motivated us to look at the sunny side of things. Not everyone knew our story, but those we confided in reassured us they were praying for us. I had shared these challenges with only a few friends; among them were prayer warriors, some of whom had faced different struggles in purchasing their homes. So, we continued praying and believing in the God who works all things for our good.

Faith brings patience when we put it into action; it allows us to remain strong in difficult times. Only God was our confidence during this season (Proverbs 3:26). Having a higher power to believe in helps to increase faith during hard times. Richard consistently commended that we needed resilience through each stage. When an offer on a house is accepted and progresses to exchanging contracts, the waiting period is painful mainly because nothing is definite that things will progress as desired. Anything can go wrong even in that last hour of signing the contracts. Our hope has got to take us through this process.

Hope alone is not adequate if we are to grow through our trials. So instead of just waiting on God, I started taking action, preparing myself to move into Dandy Mill View. One of the things I did was prepare a list of the work needed to improve the house when we moved. Mohamad Ali once said that *"lack of faith makes people fear to meet challenges."* When we allow doubt to rule in our minds, we built a set of drawbacks for action. With faith, we set free our minds and cultivate a positive mindset throughout the journey.

One's desire to deliver sometimes propels action. Through hope, we managed to keep going and believe in the situation, as it were. Therefore, whilst waiting, I started gathering plant pots and sowed some flower seeds in preparation for when we moved. I felt I shouldn't waste every challenge that came my way. For within a dark cloud, there may be a blessing and a lifting up. I could feel there was a muscle within me being strengthened in the process. Friends, all we need is to open our spiritual eyes as we walk daily as Christians. God keeps His promises when we believe, so turn on the faith and start believing. Harriet Beecher Stow warns us never to give up, for that is just the place and time that the tide will turn.

Takeaway Nuggets

1. Choose faith; it is the only anchor that holds us tight.
2. Pray for grace that takes you through the journey.
3. Talk about your fears with others.
4. Let your previous victories fuel your faith.
5. Open up about your situation and learn from the experiences of others.
6. Pay attention to what God is doing around you.
7. Affirm the things you want to see.

Chapter 8

When God is silent

Silence is the language of God, and All else is poor translation.

RUMI

There comes a time in our lives when we will seek God earnestly, a time when we will reach out and expect to receive a response from Him concerning our situation. When we pray, petitioning God for specific issues in our lives, we wait and expect a reply or breakthrough. Instead of responding, sometimes Yahweh may remain silent to our calls. Sometimes the situation worsens or leads to confusion and uncertainty as we grapple with what action to take. We found ourselves in such a place and asked ourselves whether we should continue waiting or change the course of action. At such times there is a need to determine what one wants to achieve. God does not shout out for people to trust Him; it's a personal decision.

"When God is silent, He is not still. God does some of His best work in the dark. Trust Him; He's there."

TONY EVANS

To be silent is to be quiet, not speaking or making any noise. When waiting for an answer from God, there is no sign that Yahweh is in the situation in many cases. People respond differently to the Lord's silence, and it often depends on one's level of maturity and faith in Him. When times are challenging, one tries everything one can to get a breakthrough. Then, of course, there is failure, but our Heavenly Father speaks through different ways or channels.

We must understand that God's silence is not influenced by:

- Market factors,

- What people say or,

- Financial status.

Some people choose to be still until they hear a word of prophecy about their situation. Others may keep praying or give up starting something else. Some will ask God "why", while others seek to find peace in their circumstances. Whatever decision one takes, I know that it's not an easy position to find oneself in. It is a dark and scary place with no clear direction to follow.

Many people have suffered breakdowns from stress and fear, while others have walked away from God, believing He does not exist or is not concerned about their issues. Usually, when challenges come along, our first port of call may be to call on the One who created us. For some, looking for a solution on how to come out is the best way. Christians always look to God for their solution, but it doesn't mean they get an answer immediately. It may take a year, five years or a decade for things to come to pass. At times this silence from God may threaten to overwhelm us. Our family decided to choose faith over fear as we went through this challenging season. It became a stage for us to submit to the will of our Heavenly Father, no matter how uncomfortable it was.

Listen carefully

> *"Listening is the beginning of prayer."*
> MOTHER THERESA

History has it that God is not found in noises. He desires to speak to us in prayer and silence. Mother Theresa encourages us to listen in silence because when the heart is full of other things, it is difficult to hear the voice of God. We thought God had gone silent as we went through the different phases of lockdowns due to the pandemic. We got to a point where we couldn't find an alternative house to buy after dropping the initial house. No new houses were coming on the market. We waited on God to give us the go-ahead on the decision, even though He seemed silent. It was hard to understand the meaning of it all and what God wanted us to draw from his silence.

"Don't say God is silent when your bible is closed."
UNKNOWN

As Christians, we should read God's word and understand how He operates in certain situations. When we understand, we can then pray with direction from the bible verses. Reading the Word helps us to meditate and understand how it relates to our situations. Sometimes we need to find ourselves first, and God will then find us in new ways. We can also choose to be silent during those times. If we observe silence with an expectation to hear from God, we will most likely see the reality of God's position in our lives.

We took time to go out for walks and sit alongside the canal bench to meditate. It was usually quiet in the late afternoons around the area, and investing in this time to reflect in silence helped us. Psalm 46:10 states, *"Be still and know that I am God; I will be exalted among nations, I will be exalted in the earth." (NIV)* To "be still" means to be calm, to be at peace with your circumstances. The Word of God tells us that there will be a time when we will need to be at peace, especially when we have done all that we can. We would have prayed and fasted until there is nothing to do but down our tools, thank the Almighty for the experience, and wait on Him. When God is silent, it may be an excellent time to consider serenity, and we can only do this by surrendering to the Creator's directions in our lives.

Remaining still was not an easy thing for us to do. By yielding, we choose to give everything, our power, efforts, actions and responsibilities to our heavenly Father, choosing to wait on Him for instructions. The above verse ends with a promise of victory for Yahweh, a promise to help us accomplish our tasks, hopes and aspirations once we submit. We will no longer have to direct anything; God will be in control. Therefore, my family and I needed to trust and believe that God was in control of our situation even though He was silent. David said, *"For God alone my soul waits in silence; from him comes my salvation." (Psalm 62:1, NIV).*

Draw nearer to God

Yahweh's silence can mean different things. It can be that He wants us to understand our situation better; it could be that we have prayed enough or that He is in the process of putting our package together. We may never know God's mind when He is silent, but when we don't seem to get immediate answers, we must go back and examine how we are praying. Some prayers may need us to top them up with action by considering setting goals to improve how one prays. It's critical to set goals if we want to obtain results in prayer.

We can set our goals based on how we want to improve the way we pray. From my experience, having gone through difficult seasons in my life, I have learnt to pray with direction. Setting a goal gives one a course of action to follow; it is a way of taking some responsibility. Even though God is silent; this is not a confirmation that nothing is coming; it's only a delay. So, we set a goal to come together at 3 pm daily, take a walk and pray over our situation.

In 1 Thessalonians 5:17, the Bible encourages us to pray without ceasing, an inspiration that instructs us to pray anytime, even when God seems silent. Taking time to pray without stopping is an act of accelerating our request before God in various ways:

- It helps us draw near to God (James 4:8). Second, as we move nearer, we make a shift in the shape and form of our prayers.

- It is a time to hold a fast for many people, whilst for others, there is a need for midnight petitions.

For Daniel in the Bible, it was a time to pray and offer thanks-giving three times a day (Daniel 6:10). Teachers of the Word have often encouraged holding all-night vigils, taking your petitions to a higher level. Others have recommended finding people to pray with under such difficult times. However, what matters the most is discerning what God's silence means in your particular situation.

Our family decided that we should wait on God and continue to lift our petitions to Him. It was a time to focus on the way forward as we prayed. We, therefore, chose to fast once a week in addition to praying. Ephesians 6:18 encourages Christians to always pray in the spirit with every kind of prayer and petition. When we pray in the spirit, we can perceive the will of God for our situation; however, it requires a different level of faith. As we increase our prayers and adopt different ways of praying, He will speak through His spirit. The Holy Spirit speaks through any available channel, so we must learn to listen in silence because if our hearts are full of other things, we may not hear God's voice. Paying attention is key.

Many people have confirmed that God's silence to our petitions is usually unsettling because we have always wanted to get things the easy way. We take it for granted that we will get an immediate response to our prayers, and we get worried if that doesn't happen. As a result, we forget to make sacrifices and continue seeking the face of Yahweh with trust. Isaiah 55:8 tells us that God's ways are not like ours; how we view a situation is different from how God sees it. When we think Yahweh is silent, He has not forgotten. We are challenged to be mature Christians who look to understand how God operates more positively. God is never quiet, we may not get our response as quickly as we want, but He is concerned about our welfare; He cares about our pain.

Our failure to understand how the Maker of the universe delights in speaking to us should not be the reason for a negative conclusion. Therefore, once we feel disturbed, our view of Yahweh must change to allow us to feel His compassion. Being silent may be a way for God to help us through the emotions of stress, pain, hurt and brokenness. We must heal from these first, so we can continue praying meaningfully. More so, God wants us to deal with the emotions so that we can focus on thanksgiving when we get our breakthrough. As a family, we chose to draw closer to God through our conversations with Him, seeking to feel His presence embracing us. Our association with Him sustains us through difficulties.

Sometimes God's silence brings to question His existence, especially where our faith is not that strong. When we pray, we believe that we are speaking to our Father in heaven and that he will answer our prayers. We experience Yahweh's proximity to us many times, yet sometimes we don't. When we don't get a response from God, we begin to question, *"Is God there? If He is, why is He not saying anything?"* We felt as if God had travelled somewhere far away on holiday, leaving us alone. Some teachers of the Word teach us that Yahweh wants to connect with us at that very moment when we are questioning His whereabouts. Therefore, we must be open to the connection and allow it to flow through us.

Do not fear

In the garden of Eden, Adam and Eve had sinned and went in hiding. When they heard God's voice asking, "where are you?" they did not respond by stating where they were. Instead, they said that they heard God coming and were afraid (Genesis 3:8-9). Similar circumstances happen when we venture into projects that fail and leave us grieving and heartbroken. We may find ourselves scared and move away from the connection we have with our Creator. Never abandon a project out of fear. Seek to work on your fears, and you will rise again.

Sometimes people lose focus because of how things turned out such that they miss the presence of Yahweh along the journey. However, Jehovah can still look for us at that time and ask, "Where are you?" When He asks, we should respond confidently, telling Him how we feel because we realise the Divine Father was never silent.

There are times when we are afraid to respond to God confidently. People display fear differently; they get depressed, freeze, or go in hiding, amongst many other things. In many instances, we all get paralyzed with despair, or the flight or fight mode disappears. We can then turn and throw ourselves to God, seeking peace from the storms of our life.

We should feel free to ask the Eternal Father some questions as well. Our family made sure to meditate on the Word of God in the crisis and to stand on it to bring the peace and freedom we needed. A word in season most times brings hope, and we must ask for this. Having a Rhema word means one has a strategy for silencing the negative thoughts about the absence of the Lord in a dilemma. Once we bring positivity in our prayers, fear disappears.

In many cases, people neglect to read the Word of God to know His mind when He is quiet. Reading the Bible usually takes the place of prayer when one cannot offer any requests. In addition, spending time analysing scriptures sometimes gives us a clue concerning our Maker's position in our circumstances. For example, the Prophet Habakkuk questioned God when he went through trials, *"OH Yahweh, how long shall I cry for help, and you will not hear? Or cry to you, "Violence" and You will not save?"* (Habakkuk 1:2, NIV). Habakkuk appeared to have been in a crisis, and his words are emotional.

When we think God is mute, it may be because we are anxious. We must unmute with prayer, pleading over our anxieties. Once we stop worrying about the Maker's presence, we can pray for the right decisions to flow. Sometimes we have that boldness that helps us to carry on. What if one's faith is being tested to think and feel that God is absent? God can often test our belief through His silence, and we often think He is absent. If we choose to walk with God, we must trust him without any doubt.

We took time to read the Bible and understand that the battle did not belong to us; it belonged to the Almighty. Then, we ensured that everyone understood that we had to take our position and stand still, worshipping God. Our responsibility is to do what is required within our capabilities. Our daughter would sum up with the song, "Give me the song; the praises and the utterances for my situation."

Our Heavenly Father knows what's best for us, and He is careful to prepare a complete package for us to that end. Similarly, God is always preparing us for our breakthrough. As His children, we may have feared the hurdles experienced in the past and closed ourselves off, believing that God was unavailable. Yet God requires us to tell Him exactly where we are with our decisions, or we will not see Him working in our circumstances. Once we become focused on their prayers, Yahweh will prepare us for the miracle that lies ahead.

God always has good intentions for His children; we must maintain an expectant attitude even when He seems quiet. We, therefore, encouraged and prepared ourselves to have our desires fulfilled even when we thought that God is unavailable. Doing this enables our prayers to reveal a spiritual understanding of the meaning in God's stillness. By faith, we must be ready to receive what was promised. I pictured my family walking around the place of fulfilment of our vision; however, it would come through unexpected means. The idea that we see things ahead in the now; helps us become certain that victory is on the way even when God appears quiet.

Walking towards the accomplishment of our goals requires a certain level of understanding of who we are. If we believe that we are children of the Almighty, we know from experience how we have previously received beautiful gifts from Him. That knowledge brings enlightenment on how to handle similar situations in the future. Our exposure taught us various things, that even as we wait to hear from God, we can begin to do certain things. We learned to manage resources, and everyone prioritised their jobs and other things around them. Everything became clear as we continued to bring purpose into our lives to take us to our destiny.

When we journey through a season, we must understand it from the starting point of the trip. Most people need evidence that they will get to their destination, such as a ticket. Others will commit to getting to the destination no matter what. Some people think when God has not sent any sign, something must be wrong; their argument is based on the belief that Yahweh cannot be quiet during their journey. Therefore, they expect Him to keep them company and give gifts along the way to their destination. However, might it also be that one might have embarked on the journey alone, without the Creator's involvement when there is no sign? Our Heavenly Father, in this case, maybe asking, "where are you going?"

In Genesis 16:8-9, Hagar encountered the angel near a spring in the desert while fleeing from her mistress Sarai. The angel asked; where are you coming from, and where are you going? Hagar replied to the first question only, which showed that she didn't know where she was going. Sometimes God sees that we have taken ourselves into a desert, and we don't know where we are going. So, He may be watching and saying nothing to teach us a lesson. Every season has a beginning and an end. So, we know where we are coming from, where we want to go and what we are trying to overcome.

Sometimes if we are left alone, we may come up with alternative solutions to our problems. Our family decided to come together, examine our situation, and consider if there were alternative solutions. We discussed how far we had come and what obstacles we faced, then looked at options available should our plans not work. It helped in facilitating healing and recovery caused by the pains of thinking that we had failed. When we consider alternatives, we feel good, and we can do other things while we wait.

God sees when we lack the confidence to carry on. Spiritually everybody is asked the same question at some point in their lives:

"Where are you in your walk with God today?"

"How confident are you that God has not left you alone".

We need our spiritual eyes and ears to open to hear and see things in the spiritual realm. The moment we start processing these things, we can be assured of Yahweh's position in that season. God never makes a mistake in His plans for our life. If we can be confident that our Father in Heaven loves us, we can be assured that He is working behind the scenes.

During our house buying journey, everything got muddled up, and we ended up in serious need. We were left with nothing, no house to live in and no house to buy. Despite the prayers offered and the dreams and visions we had, we got to a point where we believed that God was on mute, saying nothing. We were in a dilemma that caused many worries. Yet the Psalmist sang that *"though I walk in the valley of the shadow of death, I fear no evil; for you are with me. Your rod and Your staff comfort me"* (Psalm 23:4, NIV). Reading this brought us to the knowledge that, like Hagar God would redirect us. The angel told Hagar to go back and submit to her mistress, which she did. It was not time to move yet; Hagar understood this and obeyed.

Our lives as Christians are not our own; we must submit to God's will for our lives even though we may be at our lowest point. When our Father in Heaven is silent, there is a reason for His silence. Perhaps He wants to reroute us to a different direction, or maybe the destination is not yet ready for us. We learned not to be afraid but instead remain standing and hope for greater things when God responds. It was a case of waiting for the fullness of time. The Almighty is a God of an appointed time. He is there on time to do what needs to be done.

Takeaway Nuggets

1. God needs your trust to give you the best.

2. Silence from God does not mean denial.

3. Work on your options; it brings patience.

4. Choosing to listen is choosing to pray.

5. March around the walls of your challenge without fear but with the hope of receiving a miracle.

6. God always wants to draw our attention.

7. See everything in the spiritual realm; the battle was won before it started.

Chapter 9
There is always a lesson to learn

"Every season is one of becoming, but not always one of blooming. Be gracious with your ever-evolving self."

B. OAKMAN

Every season comes with new experiences. It is up to those going through the season to turn the experiences around for their benefit. Our church Pastor Ian, once illustrated how we learn from our past experiences by giving an example of the rear-view mirror. Everything we experience takes us back to past events as if looking at these events through a rear-view mirror. As we look back, we can evaluate and consider our present situation and then forge ahead. There are always great takeaways made up of some blessings and lessons learnt as part of our growth when we move on. Our journey through life allows us to acquire new knowledge continuously. The best thing we can do for ourselves is to choose to grow in wisdom and never remain the same.

Our biggest lesson in this period was understanding the seasons of life. Our lives centre on periodical cycles that we must master; we must know when to act, pause, push, or pull. The same applies to opportunities presented to us during seasons; we can grab them and let things spin. Our family needed to grab some of the opportunities that came with this phase. As we desired to pull through from the winter season, we found ourselves in Spring; we were not going to give up. We could easily have opted to abandon the search and rent a house for a while; renting appeared to be the easiest option at this stage. However, after weighing our options, we decided we could not miss this opportunity. The UK market was favourable to home buyers during the pandemic season as the government had waived stamp duty tax for a year.

One needs to be careful to keep an eye on each phase and be ready to act accordingly. We do not wish what happened to us on any of our friends and family. We can all avoid falling into the same predicament by learning how seasons are symbolic.

Here are some of the lessons we learnt throughout the experience:

1. Spiritual Growth

My grandmother used to tell me that every season presents many opportunities, lessons, and messages. From this background, my understanding that God also works in seasons led me to ask myself questions. I asked how to handle each situation; what actions can I take to achieve the best outcome?

From a spiritual point of view, I would ask the Almighty questions like:

- "What do you want me to learn from this" instead of "why am I going through this?"

- Lord, what do you want me to do after this storm?

These were questions asked as part of a daily exercise. Through such questions, we believed that hope differed made the heart sick. We felt that we needed something to lean on.

When facing challenges, asking oneself questions is helpful. When we seek to know the lessons we learn from a situation, we can grow every day. We remain alert or awake during the journey to not miss anything related to our destiny. We must never forget that we are masters of our destinies; although we may sometimes fail to manage our circumstances and surroundings, the way we react is always within our command.

- **Keep holding on to God and your vision.**

It became clear that God can bless us abundantly; however, we need to utilise the blessings and understand that the devil is the enemy of our progress; he will be attacking from behind. He is always fighting to snatch that which God has handed to us. As God had given my family the opportunity and the finance to buy a house, I knew that Satan wanted to frustrate us. He does this by trying to snatch our blessing so we would be disappointed and give up.

- **Guard your mouth against speaking negatively**

There's power in our words, and the devil anticipates our talk. Our family knew that we should never give him a chance because he would use our words against us. Before the storm, we used to mourn and murmur about situations negatively. Usually, when we worry or feel bitter and hate our lifestyle, there's a likelihood of speaking resentfully. However, we realised we had no basis for speaking negatively because we were already in the situation. We, therefore, kept ourselves motivated by speaking positive words which brought hope and happiness in us. We used the same affirmations mentioned in chapter 7 to help us focus on positive words.

Our speech can make and define us, or it can destroy us and our dreams. We can create or destroy things by our words. Being still and avoiding talking much renews one's spirit. The same applies when we block out the things we shouldn't hear while in the valley. Avoid listening to or reading what does not help your situation. We avoided situations that would expose us to unhelpful stories and being around negative people. The central focus is to trust God's report about the situation and to refuse any negative thoughts.

- **Mind your thoughts**

> *"Your thoughts are powerful; make them positive."*
> LOLLY DASKAL

We learn to think in unlimited conditions of victory and prosperity. Think through the good things that God has done. We choose to adopt positive or negative thinking; the power to succeed through our thoughts lies within us.

- **Know the source of your provision and seek help**

As we embarked on our journey to acquire a bigger house, we appreciated that we needed help. We had started with God; therefore, we needed to carry on believing in His promises of provision. Jehovah is the provider of our every need, be it foodstuffs, protection, love, shelter, peace, or hope (Matthew 7:9-11). The Creator confirms that He will fulfil His promises to us (James 1:17). We had been given so many opportunities in life. We had to remember that it was our duty to embrace them and act.

God guarantees to be with us in each situation. However, sometimes, it's easy to put everything else aside to concentrate on ourselves and our challenges when things get tough. We became aware that our help was from God, who would deliver an opening for us to achieve our goal in our situation. We rested on the assurance that the Almighty was with us regardless of the nature of our journey.

- **Understand that God is always with you**

Our creator will not leave those who draw close to Him. Knowing that God was always with us boosted and transformed our prayer life; we needed to step up our faith. God is always there with us; we do not have to make a Zoom call to talk to Him. Nothing could stop us from praying because we had a lot of time for praying or we could take a walk from the house. Such times brought moments of gratitude and solitude with God through prayer and quiet times of reflection.

Jacob, in the Bible, wrestled with an angel. He declared not to let the angel go until he received his blessing. Our worship needed to be aggressive in some way for us to receive our deliverance quickly. Our attitude became positive, dwelling on the fact that our Father is capable. The onus was on us to believe for our miracles.

- **Stay focused**

Where there is a man to pray, there is a God to answer, and there is a flow of abundance when He answers. To be on the battlefield to receive a miracle calls for one to remain focused. Never take your attention away. Think through what you can do in line with your vision; where can you go and get information or what is needed. We must play our part through praise and never allow anything or anyone to silence us.

Our family needed to pray and guard what God had already given us, waiting to be delivered. As children of God, we have permanent access to Him with no "ifs" nor "buts." Furthermore, renewing our confidence assists us in getting rid of the troubles, and we become bold and courageous. Through this, we can pray without ceasing.

- **Push**

> *"When fighting to possess, one can either be a loser or a winner."*
>
> ANDREW BRYAN

By prayer, we can enter the presence of God anytime. Miracles do not just come to us; we must do our part. In Matthew 15:21-28, a woman kept pleading with the king, which is the same with our prayers. When God has promised something, we must pray until we receive it. When it comes to praying, always PUSH:

- **P**ray
- **U**ntil
- **S**omething
- **H**appens

We must never be lazy to pray for our life issues; never quit the battle of blessings. Our family chose to be winners through prayer. Winning comes with going on the knees and calling God. As we do so, He grants strength and victory. Jehovah loves us and bestows honour and favour on us without holding anything back.

- **Identify a sign**

As Christians, we need to identify a sign that our Father is with us; we can ask for a particular cue from Him. For example, God provided

Noah with a rainbow signal in the Bible to indicate that He is faithful to keep His promises (Genesis 9:14-14). Given the delays and misinformation in our house situation, we were afraid, but we trusted God and remembered His promises. The creator knows us; He will not give us any bad gifts but hope and confidence that what He had started with us He would finish. Having peace within our hearts, we would share this belief as a family at every stage.

- **Know the word for your season**

God gives us a word in season during our times of trouble that we can hold onto and pray with during our challenges. It speaks into our season; it acts as a guide for us to achieving His plans and executing them for our benefit. As we went through the journey, we began to look for scriptures that spoke to our situation and life. We studied the Bible daily to find what God was saying to us through His word. Getting to know the Word produces the right emotions and powerful thoughts. Through this daily devotion, everyone in our house concluded that 2020 was the year we read the Bible most. Reading the Word from the Bible made us stand firm and trust the Lord more. Get a specific verse for you and your situation to keep you going. We can also praise and ask Jehovah for wisdom and understanding, helping us move forward whilst building on our strength.

- **Shake off unpleasant things**

Through spiritual growth, God builds our character, and one can see the depth of grace offered. Sometimes the Creator has a way of deconstructing things in us. Our characters can be filled with unpleasant stuff, which is not helpful in particular seasons, such as envy, jealousy, lies, anger, or any negative thoughts. A particular phase in life sometimes demands that we fend off such things. For us, flourishing spiritually meant shaking off undesirable characteristics and developing a pleasing personality before the Almighty. One can ask if this will be helpful to achieving any personal goals? If not, it's time to change and remain inspired as one seeks maturity.

Under challenging times, it's easy to be anxious or worried over things we have no control over. We struggled to contain such feelings, but eventually, we realised that we could let go and release them into God's hands. In return, we took back God's promises according to 1 Corinthians 10:13 *"there is no temptation beyond what one can cope with except such is common to man; but God is faithful who will not allow you to be tempted beyond what you are able". (NIV)*

We are encouraged to forgive where it demands us. Going through challenges requires being gentle with others. Our challenges bring us to the training ground where we must learn to forgive. We mustn't allow the load of grievances and grudges we carry to affect our road to success. The noblest thing to do is to forgive, forget and move on.

- **Be patient**

> *"There is something good in all seeming failure. You are not to see that now. Time will reveal it. Be patient."*
> Swami Sivananda

We learnt patience and believed that He who promised would fulfil. When one is encouraged to be patient, it does not mean they will not focus on the issue. It means that they will be cautious and expectant. The Christian religion is not theory but is revealed through practical living. If we are to be faithful children of God who become successful in our walk with Him, we must exercise patience in everything. Endurance brings the hope that takes us to the finishing line; we can believe that we will hold what we are expecting to receive with persistence.

- **Always be content**

> *"We need much less than we think we need."*
> Maya Angelou

Many times, we ask how one can be content when experiencing difficult and painful issues. If we look closely, we can find some moments of joy in our storms, and these are the ones we can embrace and celebrate. We can rejoice as we walk blameless, choosing to see only the good. The idea is to be able to move forward without weeping.

We refused to make the problem bigger than it was but to find some things we could appreciate and celebrate through praise. An appreciative spirit turns all that it touches into happiness. Jehovah opened our eyes by doing so, and we began finding joy in the simple things like sunshine, good meals, family, and friends.

2. Fellowshipping With Others

We live life as if we are running a race, and we try to do it alone. It is unusual for one to run a marathon alone. In any endeavour, we need helpers and cheerleaders along the way. In every man's walk of life, he needs people to walk alongside him. For His children, God always raises destiny helpers, and He appoints and entrusts them to assist us to accomplish our purposes. These are people, opportunities, or things that God uses to facilitate the process of taking us out of our trials.

• Identify your destiny helpers

God uses individuals as conduit pipes and raceways to disburse help on the planet. Every person in the universe will need a vision helper at some point in their pursuit of life. No man is an island unto himself. Our creator sent out great destiny helpers during our house buying season. Some of them advised us from their experiences, while others provided food, shelter, and comfort. Sometimes when we think about such powerful men and women who sacrificed their finances, including precious material things for us, we are short of words. A mere thank you would not suffice. Always appreciate those who walk with you in your journey.

- **Reach out to others if you can**

*"Sometimes reaching out taking someone's hand is the
beginning of a journey; at other times it is allowing
another to take yours."*

VERA NAZARIAN

We believed that we should pray and ask God for good people to walk the journey with us. Sometimes one can hang around people who easily forget about them when faced with storms of life. We concluded that we needed men and women who had been through similar experiences and came through the other side. These are the people who could walk with us and not be weary; they would not give up before time but help us cope with the challenges of that season.

The friends we reached out to had not been through a similar situation to ours, but their previous experience of challenges helped them to encourage us. They shared advice and prayed with us. They understood what it felt like to be in need and in a time of uncertainty. Our family might have ended up sleeping on the streets had we not reached out to others. Speaking to someone may bring a solution to the problem, enabling us to handle the situation better. However, we must be careful, as not everyone we offload to can help.

A time came when we had to set pride and shame aside to let our families know about the state of our affairs. It was not easy, especially for me, but it worked. I had always fought through my challenges alone. I would weep in my closet and encourage myself, always believing that hard times never kill. I have always gone before God with every worry, and He provided a solution. However, this challenge was different; it affected everyone; we had not faced such a mammoth challenge before.

Sharing our concerns with those close to us somewhat took the bulk of the burden off our shoulders. We thank God for Zoom, WhatsApp, Facebook, and other communication platforms we used to communicate with family and friends in that season. As a result, our moments of loneliness were minimised.

• Re-evaluate yourself

My family and I had never gone through such a problem before. In my 18 years of relocating to the United Kingdom, I'd had accommodation. During my time at University, I never had to worry about where to stay. Through the house buying experience, we learned that life will not always remain the same. Perhaps this was now time to re-evaluate some of our ideals. Usually, men fall short when they show pride and confidence in their wisdom and abilities. Proverbs 16:18 reminds us that pride goes before destruction. We must therefore be careful not to stumble as we try to do the right thing. Taking time to re-examine oneself brings new strategies and increases energy levels.

• There is no loss in giving

> *"Giving always benefits two people, the giver and the receiver."*
> DUNCAN THOMPSON

We experienced the power of giving as beneficiaries of other people's generosity. It was amazing to witness people's generosity, giving up their living space to accommodate us; indeed, giving is a virtue. Some people give not because they have more than enough but because they find it a noble thing to do; they sacrifice for a need.

There are different levels of giving:

- Financial giving
- Giving of time in the form of listening, giving knowledge and encouragement.
- Showing love.

We read in Luke 6:38 that *"when we give, it shall be given back to us in good measure; pressed down, shaken together, and running over.*

For with the same measure, it shall be given to us. "(NIV). That said, people should not give and expect that they will get the same thing back in larger quantities. We now know and believe that some people give simply from the goodness of their hearts.

Most people who gave to us during our predicament are not relatives; some were not even close to us. They found it prudent to give without looking back. When we give, we get more; prosperity is sometimes linked to the law of giving. To whom much is given, more is expected (Luke 12:48). This principle can never go wrong if applied through serving God. To be successful in life, we must give and give more. Not everyone is a giver; many find it hard to part with their hard-earned cash or belongings. Yet, as we became recipients of others' generosity, we learnt that we could also be a blessing to others in different ways.

Through meditating on prayer, we decided to show grace to others during our trial. We made a list of people we thought would appreciate and benefit from someone's support. I contacted the national prayer group coordinator of a prayerline which I sometimes attend and picked ten women I had never met before. They were going through challenges that ranged from unemployment to health issues. Later, it so happened that I received a financial gift on my birthday, and with a grateful heart, I shared the money between the ten ladies.

I could not have commemorated my birthday in 2020 in a better way than through giving. Once I did that, I felt good. My family were touched when I shared the news with them, and we mutually decided to give away our monthly travel and clothing expenditure for the lockdown period. In addition, we nominated a charity for the deaf and dumb in Zimbabwe and sent money for food parcels, and it became one of the ways to share our family blessing with others. We can never stop sowing good seeds during tough times.

- **You are not the only one going through a challenge**

As each day passed, we witnessed that family was everything; being there for each other and moving together was a blessing. When we appreciate that, we can enjoy our relationships. It brought peace and contentment in knowing that we were all as one and God was preparing something better for us. From watching the news on TV and reading on the internet, we realised that many other people were going through even worse challenges, making our situation easier to bear. We were still family; we moved together with a fighting spirit even after the challenging season. God preserved us.

- **Provoke your miracle**

> *"We are in control of our own heaven or hell."*
> MARIE WALTERS

Going through a difficult time in life should not stop us from carrying other people's burdens through prayers. This commitment to offering petitions for others encouraged us to consider other people's storms despite our own. Once we do so, we obtained a legal ground to challenge God in our prayers, reminding Him of our good works. We provoked a breakthrough because some miracles happened as we stood beside others sharing their pain and grief. To receive our breakthrough, we need to challenge that by our faith.

3. Personal Growth

- **Don't settle for less**

When tests in life come, it is sometimes easier to settle for less than what we want; this was evident in our situation once we abandoned the first house. Starting afresh was not an easy option as there was nothing on the market to meet our criteria. At the same time, we were under pressure, as we could not stay with our dear friends forever. We almost settled for houses we didn't want out of desperation. We needed to be principled as we sought to make the right decisions for us, and so we had to be honest, disciplined and stay within the boundaries of our checklist.

It was not a smooth sail, especially when we have been through such a crisis. It would have been easier to give up on our dreams and settle for less. Therefore, I urge you to hold on to your beliefs and enjoy each moment. Anything that takes away one's time, or joy is not good. Always make it a point to manage every stage well.

- **Count your blessings**

After all had been said and done, we were left with so many after-thoughts. Some incidents called for us to sit down to reflect and share the lessons learnt for our growth. We cherished and enjoyed these moments as they grounded and forced us to spend quality time together. From that time, it has become routine for our family to come together once a month and discuss individual and household issues. These are some of the blessings we are grateful for.

Takeaway Nuggets

1. Grow physically, grow spiritually, grow mentally.

2. Get ready for what life will teach you and be receptive to the lessons in every way.

3. Our mistakes may sometimes take us where there is innovation.

4. No one has ever been poor by giving, give generously.

5. Be nice to other people.

6. Take a deep breath and listen to the teachings and embrace them.

7. Reflect upon your blessings.

Chapter 10

Reflections

Honest reflection opens your mind to reprogramming,
change, success and freedom.

UNKNOWN

Self-reflection is good for promoting self-development and growth. Psychologists agree that looking back at past events assists in bringing clarity and making life more meaningful. I love Soren Kierkegaard's quote, *"Life can be understood backwards; but it must be lived forwards."* We all learn from experience; reflections bring transformation connected to individual values and goals. Our reflections are based on mindful deliberation and scrutiny of beliefs and actions for learning.

When one reflects, they evaluate where they are now against where they want to be in the future, including the steps needed to get there. By doing so, they can find meaning in our struggles. As we reflect on our journeys, we see some of the mistakes we made along the way. Reflection is good practice that allows us to grow, have faith, and humble ourselves, teaching us valuable lessons. Reflection assists us to critically review our actions and decisions and consider where we need to improve.

For children of God, taking time to reflect also helps us get to a place where we forgive those who hurt us in the process, and we can apologise to those we wronged. Jim Manney in his book, "a simple, life-changing prayer," talks about a life-changing prayer where our faith takes us to a place to examine and convict ourselves. It is this conviction that will finally allow us to make things right with God as we confess and ask Him to forgive us and help us find peace. Unfortunately, not everything we do leaves us in a better place regarding our relationship with the Almighty. Sometimes we find ourselves embroiled in sin because we are trying to achieve something good. It's important to remember that we always learn from our mistakes, which prepare us for the future.

As we reflected on our journey, we saw how some aspects of our lives had improved during our challenges, especially our walk with God. I could see His Word coming alive and thriving all over our lives.

Create space to reflect

"The journey to self-love and self-acceptance must begin with self-examination."
IYANLA VANZANT

Once we moved into the house, we took time to settle in and recover mentally and physically. We finally had the opportunity to have conversations whilst relaxed and look at things with clear minds. Reviewing our journey opened our eyes, and we could look at the future from different lenses. Looking back provided us with the opportunity to appreciate what we had achieved; we could now see the miracle around us.

God's love for man allows Him to direct the course of history in a manner that we, as mortals, do not understand. Recalling where we'd been a few years before when we lived in a rented house to purchasing our first property made us see how far we'd progressed and how much God had provided for us by His grace. Although the idea of taking time to reflect on the odyssey may seem an easy process, ours was not simple. Initially, we were reluctant to look back because of the painful memories of the events. Fortunately, we did not feel the pain but joy because what we received was better than what he had before. We couldn't believe that we finally got a house.

Upon reflection, our journey was an interesting one. There were other things to celebrate too, mainly the transformation, including growth as individuals and our relationships. Of course, there were disappointments too, like the stress, the viewings and not knowing the truth, among many others. However, had we not gone on this life-transforming journey, we wouldn't have known about its impact on our lives. Ruth Chambers said, "until you take the journey of self-reflection, it is almost impossible to grow or learn life."

We did some self-introspection individually and as a family. Sometimes specific experiences leave us without a purpose in life. Seth Igbo said that we must ask ourselves questions regularly to remain focused, in check and fulfilled. Milton Kamwendo reminds us to question everything; question your current outcomes and question your evidence. He encourages us to question our own beliefs and limitations too. We must ask whether things go wrong for quality control and to help us grow and shed off some unwanted things in our lives. Honesty with ourselves is needed if we are to grow gracefully.

Andrew Bryant inspires us to ask questions that shift us towards a solution or where we can tap into resources. As an individual, I asked myself the following questions:

- How did I behave during the process as Rujeko, as a wife and a mother?

- Am I living true to myself, or am I taking anything for granted?

- Is there anything I have learnt or improved on?

- What is this asking of me?

It was liberating for us as a family to realise where we stood in our relationships. Of course, we all need relationships to grow, but sometimes things happen that affect these relationships. In other situations, we take our relationships for granted, which may cause us to drift apart. What is important is that we should take care of our relationships just as we care for ourselves.

Wake up to achieve

"Everything in your life is a reflection of a choice you have made. If you want a different result, make a different choice."

ANONYMOUS

When we reflect, we expose ourselves to taking action. We can identify things that worry us and deal with them. For example, we are often worried about our failure to achieve the goals we set. When we reflect, we expose our brains to the highest level of thinking. Having gone through what we went through, we could not afford not to reflect on the journey. We identified the positives and negatives of our experience. From then on, we knew what was good for us and what to discard.

Although the process took over ten months, in the end, it felt like it happened over a short time; the sorrow, pain and running around could easily have happened in 48 hours. Therefore, the fundamental question to ask was, "could we do this again given another opportunity?" As time passed, we could respond with a yes; we would do it again. Asking such questions helped us see things more clearly.

We documented every detail of our journey in a diary every day. Jennifer Porter once wrote an article about why we should take time for self-reflection. She recommended selecting a reflection that matches one's preferences. Our diary was one of the best things we did, and we journaled our feelings. Journaling is one way people can reflect on what is going on in their lives. As we reviewed our writings, we realised that what was behind this experience was our desire to do better in life. As we moved a step up, we understood that everything happened because we wanted to achieve and take the necessary action. We now see an improved lifestyle, the aftermath of our experience. We have a beautiful home in an area we never thought we would afford. These are the results of hard work and tenacity. We are in a better place because of this journey. We must never be afraid to take the plunge.

Our adventure and its transition story remind me of the transfiguration of Jesus (Mark 9:2-9). The Bible says that Jesus changed in appearance, which I noticed happened in our experience. Jesus appeared, dazzling white; that's who He became even after His death.

We changed in many ways; what evolved in our case was:

- Our inward appearance,

- The environment we lived in,

- Our emotions and strength,

- Our friends and acquaintances.

People change emotionally as they express feelings such as sadness, happiness, or anger. Acknowledging the transformations taking place in us brought fulfilment and truth about our lives. The way we did things changed, although we cannot put the finger on it. The challenges we face in life change us, and people can see the evidence around us. We felt and saw these changes as we reflected.

Talking about our experiences can bring painful and sad memories yet looking back can also bring healing and the appreciation of what we have been through. John C Maxwell reminds us that reflective thinking turns experience into insight. Seeing the strides of success we'd made, we experienced restoration within our emotions. Where we are now, we can speak from a good place of contentment, hope and self-actualisation.

> *"Don't look in the mirror to comb your hair, instead*
> *check out in the mirror to focus on yourself."*
> ANONYMOUS

When we use the mirror to reflect this way, we progress and become the person we want to be. In addition, it helps us in building and maintaining healthy relationships. As humans, when we look in the mirror, we sometimes observe the glass, only to realise later that our bodies had deteriorated, and we even abandoned certain habits.

Christians can use the mirror to reflect on their relationship with God. As a family, we realised that our connection with the Creator remained constant going forward and allowed us to make necessary changes as we discerned what God wanted us to do to bring spiritual growth.

Acknowledging mistakes

Reminiscing on the challenges we came across as a family often led to self-judgement instead of self-reflect. Once we acknowledged specific values that came into play, we could assess our strengths and weaknesses. It helped in recreating ourselves. For example, we could have abandoned everything regarding buying the house and opted for renting. Sometimes we make excellent decisions by abandoning projects that drain our energy and time. One can conclude that the more selectively ignorant we become, the more broadly knowledgeable we can be. We see this at play when we acknowledge our mistakes without having to justify them. Without focusing on where we went wrong, we can see what has changed physically and spiritually in and around us. We were able to look back with gratitude. We are grateful that we have gone through this experience. We believe that we took great leaps of faith and did not allow fear to hold us back. What we received is the gift of perseverance.

When we make quiet reflections, there is room to take effective action. The end product of our testing time in this season of our life brought a sense of fulfilment. Our journey is now a testimony of what God has done in our lives through a challenge. Whatever we went through is the testimony of a miracle that has been fulfilled. What Yahweh said He would do is what He has done - to bless us. Whatever happened, we still have each other as a couple, and as a family, we supported each other through the tough times. Worse things could have happened; some families have broken up due to challenging times they faced. Ours has instead grown out of this challenge, we appreciate each other more, and we are progressing together. We cannot even remember all the bad experiences and arguments we had during the said time. Even where there were negative confessions, they no longer look bad because we have come through it.

Going down memory lane reveals some of the new opportunities that came out of the experience. We learn wisdom through reflections, said Confucius. This season, we have been transformed; our friendships have grown; our way of doing things has changed. Many of the changes helped us step into the future, whilst others brought an immediate revolution. We realised that we could choose to do things the right way, and we keep discovering great lessons about this season of trials. Those who learn inherit the earth, but the learned find themselves beautifully equipped for the world that no longer exists when it comes to change. We also find our purpose through reflections. The Bible in Colossians 3:10 encourages us to put on the new self, which is to be renewed in knowledge. No season is permanent. What we went through in ten months is not who we are now. Behind us is a variety of skills revealed, raised, and resurfaced.

We have improved some of our soft skills; we often prioritised self-care because we saw it as a necessity. For example, we can now take a nap during the day to think things through and refresh without feeling guilty. We never did that during our journey due to pressing issues. When we practice self-care, we are doing restorative work. Part of such work involves seeking support. This is viewed as a skill because we needed to communicate well as a family.

We can see how we negotiated through the process and communicated with the professionals to purchase our home. The essence of acceptance comes from acknowledging the situation we found ourselves in and how we managed to work through this together. We now see ourselves developing self-awareness concerning the challenges around us and acting accordingly. We can see how we managed to think more strategically, opening opportunities for ourselves and making the appropriate decisions or choices we needed to make. Having these skills carried us through the process.

Regroup, refocus and move on

The privilege of reminiscing on the past allowed us to evaluate how we handled relationships in the process. We realised that some of our friends might no longer be as close to us as they used to be. Some family members and relatives needed our support when we were facing challenges, and we couldn't be there for them. They may not know what we went through. We must consider things carefully because we can misread motives and judge ourselves too harshly. Our feelings may have been hurt during the journey, which influences us to look at things differently. We realised that sometimes facing challenges can result in communication breakdowns with loved ones. Often, people may fail to support or walk together with the one going through a difficult time. Yet, in everything, we must continue to love.

When we considered the seasons of life, we realised that we could not change the circumstances, but we could look back with hope and accept what happened as a family. We can only hope that we mastered the lessons and can carry them on to the next season. According to Isaiah 40:31, the Bible affirms that, *"Those who wait upon the Lord shall renew their strength; they will soar on wings like eagles; they will run and not be weary, they will walk and not faint" (NIV).* So, we regroup, refocus, and move forward; this is what is expected from the children of God when we have been through a period of struggles.

The Bible teaches us to pray and give thanks in everything (1 Thessalonians 5:18). During our trying moments, we found it hard to assimilate the way to give thanks in the face of our troubles. This scripture says to give thanks in *everything*, not for anything but *all* situations. Our maturity was tested through understanding the meaning of this verse. As we began to ponder offering our gratitude, we realised God wanted us to be grateful despite our challenges. To be able to praise Him within our extraordinary situation. In return, God would turn our challenges into miracles.

God can bring restoration through winter periods of life. There are so many things we lose in trying to get into the cold or heat. Usually, some trees shed off their leaves whilst some animals lose fur. Understanding that this will not remain the same is critical and is a part of the natural change process within those seasons. The trees will soon start to bud before the end of the season, and the fur will grow back.

In our time of difficulties, God will re-establish us and restore what we lost. Jehovah can make us recover years lost and help us rediscover our purpose. By receiving such grace, we can revive ourselves and bring fruitfulness. Therefore, we should still observe what the Creator is building or destroying within a particular challenge.

Some gifts are to sustain us for a particular season. Something had held us back from buying any house, and when the government lifted the first phase of the lockdown, we could have rushed to get any house. Nonetheless, we had learnt to be more careful. We kept to the plan even though we could easily have deviated from it. We could have doubted ourselves or the hand of God in our situation. It was comforting to think of how far we had come and acknowledge everything we had faced and overcame. Even though we regret overstaying with our friends, we respect and appreciate their love and hospitality.

We remained courageous and hopeful even when people lost houses in the pandemic due to different financial and health reasons. We have gained despite the problems. How wonderful is that? We offer our gratitude and thanksgiving for all that happened and those who helped us make it through.

Takeaway Nuggets

1. Always meditate at every stage in life.
2. Consider the wins, gains, losses and build a life from them.
3. Take action based on silent reflections.
4. Create life goals that are fulfilling.

5. You will always make mistakes in life, acknowledge, and learn from them.

6. Be quick to move on, don't get stuck.

7. Remain courageous.

Chapter 11

A new season is born

Just the smell of summer can make me love again.

UNKNOWN

Glory be to God in the highest.

This was the song we sang on our way to the Estate agents to collect the keys to our new house; we had made it! Finally, the house was here, and we were excited. "Life has many seasons, but they all pass," said Carroll Roberson. This, too, had come to pass. We had been fighting both a physical and spiritual battle and fighting to the end brought us victory. We had prayed and offered thanksgiving before setting off. Being wary, we also prepared ourselves for any eventuality should they tell us a different story when we arrived. However, everything was in place; when we got there, it was our time! The agent advised us that the seller was waiting at the house to hand over the keys in person. How good was that for us! It was the beginning of a new era in our lives, and we could see God's goodness and mercy following us everywhere.

Vision fulfilment

Habakkuk 2: 3, says "*for the vision is for an appointed time. It speaks to the end it will not prove false. If it seems slow, wait for it, it will certainly come; it will not delay*" (NIV). God had fulfilled our vision at the appointed time. Walking through the doors of the new house was like holding a new-born baby in our arms. We felt at home straight away. With great big sighs, we released the tension we'd carried for the previous ten months. Getting to this point, it had been a roller coaster of a ride.

To see the fulfilment of our vision after many months of waiting brought a sense of celebration; it was a time of joy and gratitude. We could not contain the joyous smiles as we opened our hearts and arms to embrace our new home. It was a moment *of out with the troubles and worries of winter and in with the summer celebrations, hot meals, entertaining and relaxing*! The months of homelessness turned into one day of praise and gratitude. We had been Nomads for almost all of 2020, and no one could have guessed that we'd end up in the same area we thought we had left for good. Nothing is permanent; God can turn a test into a testimony.

When a mother finally holds her baby after a difficult pregnancy, she will never want to hand the baby over to someone else. This is how we felt as we started planning to design the house's interior and transform it into our dream home. We went around the house, room by room, admiring everything and amazed at the decision we'd made from frustration. The house offered more than we had asked for; it was our dream house, a miracle house. What a perfect package of goodness; God is a God of abundance, not abandonment. We couldn't believe that it was now ours; indeed, we had overcome every block the winter season had tried to put in our way.

Jehovah has given us a double portion. So, we can conclude that it is possible to do some remarkable things in life no matter how dark or cold and snowy the winter may become.

Every seasonal experience brings teaching points. As a family, we have grown, gained wisdom, and we came out stronger. We cried, experienced anxieties and loneliness, but now we can put our minds to rest and enjoy our beautiful home. We know that after giving birth, the mother's body must recover, and she prepares to wear new clothes. That is what happens with everyone who goes through the process of buying a new house. Everything eventually works together, and you start dressing up the house with furniture and other accessories.

There is hope in every trial; therefore, never give up chasing your dreams.

We did not give up on our goals; we kept pressing on fighting till the end; getting the house we eventually got was a bonus. In 2 Timothy 4:7, Paul speaks about his steadfast faith and unending love for the gospel of Jesus Christ. For him to succeed in achieving his purpose after having gone through many challenges in his ministry is a lesson that life is a journey. Going through a season is only part of that journey, and Paul never quit the race. Therefore, coming out of the winter season into spring without miscarrying our objectives was empowering and exciting; it brought a sense of success and achievement.

One of my favourite Bible verses is found in Philippians 4:8, *"Finally, brothers and sisters, whatever is true, whatever is noble, whatever is right, whatever is pure, whatever is lovely, whatever is admirable--if anything is excellent or praiseworthy--think about such things."* (NIV). Whenever we encounter challenges, the best thing to do is imagine and allow yourself to think, see and feel the desired end in your mind. This exercise will motivate you to pursue your goal and remain focused on transforming and shaping your life. Our family did not dwell on the past and all our disappointments because we attained our goal.

Rebuilding

When life gets to be too much, it can sometimes be debilitating. Going through difficult challenges can affect our emotions and promote low self-esteem. One sees themselves unworthy of anything after having failed at one aspect of their objective. It is an excellent practice to deal with any pain and bad experiences that can affect us in the future. Recovering from our disappointments and failures can often be very tough. Bob Goff said, "Embrace uncertainty. Some of the most beautiful chapters in life won't have a title until much later." Rebuilding our lives starts today, right now, as we hope to place ourselves into a recovery position slowly. We can do this by choosing to rebuild and restore what we lost, taking time to build positive mindsets, and mending broken relationships.

As we enjoy owning a house, we also pursue forgiveness and healing for relationships that may have broken down while going through the challenging season. As a family or individually, we could have offended people along the way. Ephesians 4:32 tells us to be kind and to seek forgiveness with each other. Forgiveness starts with us if we are to make it effective; I took it as an opportunity to forgive myself for grieving my soul, and there was so much to forgive myself for. There were days I was uncomfortable with worry and stress, the times I didn't have enough rest, including the times we may have argued as a family. To be released and healed, we must forgive ourselves of the past with its negative feelings, emotions, and limiting beliefs.

> *"God may forgive your sins, but your nervous*
> *system won't."*
> ALFRED KORZYBSKI

Going through a new season marked the opening of a new chapter, which brings many assurances forward. So, it is encouraging to know that we can do something towards promoting a healthy body and mind in the new season. This is crucial if we are to enjoy life and make positive life choices in the future. Everything is a process. We are, therefore, taking time to have compassion for ourselves and release every negative issue that stole our peace from our minds and soul in that season. We are setting ourselves apart from everything connected to the pain experienced during the house buying process and taking responsibility. We must free ourselves from the bondage brought about by the failures and challenges we experienced, such as stress, depression, and confusion. Together we are to acquit ourselves to receive inner healing from any damaging long-term consequences. Doing all this will help us rediscover our purpose.

Many people may not be brave enough to go through the process of rebuilding on their own. Therefore, it may be helpful to reach out to someone for support, although it was not our preferred choice to speak to our doctors about mental health concerns that arose from experiencing the difficult seasons. There are other forms of support that help people come to terms with mental health or physical concerns.

Accept things gradually

One day at a time...

Usually, it takes a long time to recover from an extensive setback. Psychologists have always said that there may be many complex emotions one needs to get through to come to terms with their experience. We agreed that we take things slowly, "one day at a time." We took the time to grieve, pray and uncover some of the mistakes we made in the process. Some of the decisions we made were carried out of a genuine heart, even though they may not have been the right ones, and consequently, we had to deal with some regrets.

At a personal level, walking through the journey of forgiving myself, I realise how such choices took away the freedom from within, and I must find peace in my heart by taking responsibility for my mistakes, regrets and failings. I found a tiny basket that I had bought while on holiday just after the first lockdown. The basket looked like a jar with a lid; I wrote down every worry I had on a piece of paper and dropped it into the basket. After that, I didn't need to worry anymore. For seven days, I prayed over every worry, forgiving myself and asking God to forgive me.

"If the son has set you free, you are free indeed."
JOHN 8:36

Going through such a process brought a sense of peace and a desire to forgive. If God had already set me free, therefore I am free indeed; there was no need to condemn or blame myself for the experience. We were fortunate that our journey had a happy ending; therefore, finding joy, obtaining forgiveness, and going over the process brought much peace. Finally, I took our small incinerator and set it in the garden and burnt the little basket with its contents. It cleared my mind of all negative feelings about our previous challenges.

If we have forgiven ourselves, we should also be merciful to those around us; being considerate of their feelings and accepting them as they are. As a family, we had to forgive one another; this process required us to talk honestly to each other while accepting our different roles and responsibilities when things went wrong. Talking about it was liberating; it set us all free, and everyone felt they were no longer vulnerable. We are ready to move on and enjoy our lives without any fear or judgment from each other, and as a result, our interactions have started thriving positively.

We must appreciate ourselves to bring back happiness in our lives; this involved affirming good things about our life. Even though we have gone through some hardships, we can still appreciate and love ourselves. This experience has brought so much good in us, and we can see the better in each one of us. We cannot think of laying the blame for our bad experience on anyone. We take responsibility for part of the blame for what happened, but we love seeing the change within us. We love ourselves and all we have gone through. As we appreciate ourselves, we can affirm good things.

When we hold a baby, we take time to say a little prayer. We do this out of knowing and exercising power given to us by Christ (Luke 10:19). As we prayed for the house, we spoke life, happiness and peace. We also had to deal with every past spirit that may have inhabited the house. When one buys a house that has been lived in before, there is a need to deal with things that the previous owners did. We are aware that the owners were not believers, and the fact that the sellers sold the house due to divorce means we have to deal with the spirit of divorce. We went through a time of prayer and fasting to cleanse the house. Our petitions to God focused on declaring fruitfulness, happiness, peace, praise and worship in the house.

Look after yourself

*"Caring for your body, mind, and spirit is your greatest
and grandest responsibility. It's about listening to the
needs of your soul and then honouring them."*

KRISTI LING

We are constantly reminded to take care of ourselves after coming out of a season. Rebuilding demands an attitude of gratitude, and this flows from appreciating what we went through and seeing the end results. It is out of the abundance of the heart that our mouth speaks (Luke 6:45). When we testify to the Lord's doing in our lives, we consider every transformational work and offer gratitude allowing us to speak positively about our lives and the things we have accomplished. Thankfulness allows us to move on with hope and expectation for what the future will release to us. Every time I walk through the house, I give thanks. This is the prayer I offer out of being in awe of Jehovah's work. The new season has brought joy to our hearts. God has blessed us with a beautiful house, a wonderful family, and great friendships. We can see growth in us, and all the other things brought by this experience.

It is, therefore, a time to seek healing and restoration. When we have gone through a challenging phase, we need healing and restoration. The mind, body and spirit must heal from the aches and pains experienced. Our situation got to a point where everything was out of control, bringing stress, depression, and body aches. When this happens, one must seek to bring harmony and balance to one's mind, which passes through to the physical body. We have survived the suffering by going for massages, confronting negative thoughts, and releasing positive thinking. Some mental exercises such as meditating on Bible verses and taking walks helped to bring in refreshing times. We survived these challenging times by receiving joy from our heavenly Father; our Creator promises to restore our joy, happiness, peace, and love. And His grace is always sufficient for us.

*"Sometimes the most important thing in a whole day is
the rest we take between two breaths."*
ETTY HILLESUM

Taking care of ourselves involves looking at every aspect of our lives too. We cannot care for our loved ones if we don't take care of ourselves first. It helps us in being present in other affairs. Nowadays, we can even review our eating habits and sleeping patterns and get as much exercise as possible. Doing so means adopting organic ways of dealing with anxiety, stress and depression. Our difficult season affected our eating habits, and we realised that everyone had put on weight. We had fallen into eating anyhow to cope with the stresses. We can take some recommended measures to help reduce and even get rid of stress and anxiety with time. We now need to take on a balanced diet and maintain it. The privilege of working from home makes life better, and we can take time to relax and sleep more hours. As we do so, our bodies are restored and made whole. The onus to determine the best self-care practices for ourselves lies with us.

We must never forget that prayer changes things.

- It brings rejuvenation.
- it sets a new meaning to life,
- It promotes positive emotions.

In the process of rebuilding, we must continue offering prayers, praying for the new home and asking the Holy Spirit to come and dwell in it. I had to redecorate the house the best I could, painting it with fresh paint to mark a new phase and beginning of a new life. I was not going to take on someone's past and make it my own. Similarly, I removed all curtain poles and blinds and replaced them with new ones. I also put-up new picture frames and rebuilt the wardrobes and installed a new kitchen. Seeing the transformation was amazing while at the same time we could be assured that the past was gone. This change brought a shift of the mindset to embrace the new.

"To love oneself is the beginning of a lifelong romance."

OSCAR WILDE

Taking care of ourselves is the greatest indication of self-love. Through practising self-love, we restore ourselves and regain strength. Self-love involves knowing who you are and that you are worthy of your love, time, and respect. As a family, we needed to rediscover ourselves again after all the obstacles, exhaustion, and burnout. We love ourselves genuinely, even with the scars of our past. Never give up on yourself because of your complicated past; taking care of yourself should be a priority and should come easily. "Almost everything will work again if you unplug it for a few minutes, including you" (Anne Lamot).

In Isaiah 43:18-19, God wants us to forget our past and not rely on it because a new thing is about to be released. Yahweh confirms that He is making a way in the wilderness and streams in the wetland. We, therefore, must get ready to receive the new and not stay in the things of the past. The Covid-19 pandemic caused so much loss and pain to us as a family and individually. Therefore, we pray for divine health and detoxifying the harmful cells that cause sickness in the body. One can only be restored when they position themselves in that place for new things. Furthermore, we must deal with any form of fear to be completely restored. We are therefore going through the process of recovery whilst enjoying the new normal.

Takeaway Nuggets

1. Change is inevitable, prepare for it and get in the flow of the changes.

2. Come to terms with your past; it happened.

3. Everything takes time; your negative emotions will heal.

4. Your power; your fuel for a better future.

5. Offer gratitude for your past, present and future.

6. Uncover your freedom from rebuilding.

7. Self-healing and restoration bring everlasting growth.

Chapter 12

Conclusion

*I have fought a good fight, I have finished the race, I kept
the faith-*

2 TIMOTHY 4:7(NIV)

*"There is a time for everything and a season for every activity under
the heavens." Ecclesiastes 3:1.* All things have a season, and all seasons
must come to an end. Nothing lasts forever. Prophetess Dina Rolle
said, "Every season has an end for a harvest to begin." We see the
Spring season bringing rain and the winter coming with hardships. To
experience the benefits of the seasons, they must come to an end. In the
aftermath of every season, we begin to harvest the proceeds from that
season. My family's journey could not have remained the same because
everything lasts only for a season.

The lockdown would not remain forever; eventually, the government
had to ease the restrictions. Finally, businesses could not remain closed
forever, the season to reopen came, and people could, at last, come out.
The Government eased the lockdown in stages before finally lifting
them all off. My family also finally arrived at our destination, our new
home, and we are forever grateful for the journey, the challenges, and
the victories.

We offer our gratitude to the Creator who makes all things
beautiful. The memories of the bad experiences have started to fade; it's
unbelievable how time flies! God is a God of all seasons; it's amazing
how He works in our lives.

Having come along with me through our home buying adventure, I
believe you've had a good glance at what seasons can bring and can have
a better understanding of how they work. God is the author of our time

here on earth, and we can choose how we want to spend that time. First, however, we must be aware of time, understand it and acknowledge that things can and will change, as seasons do.

My family and I set out on a journey, and our goal was to find a new family home. Looking back, we can see that we didn't achieve the goal just like that; it came at a cost that could have taken our lives. We have learned that we must be determined to achieve our goals, which comes down to knowing the "WHY" of one's goal. One must know the benefit of their actions. *Why did we want to move house?* Our WHY fuelled our willpower to make it happen and our persistence to meeting the objective. We can now see some of the benefits of persevering. We can now conclude that it is a privilege to set a goal and accomplish it.

Find yourself

Challenges characterise every goal, and similarly, each season has its threats. We must, therefore, be ready to face the challenges associated with each season. Our problems may not necessarily be the same, but some strategies to overcome them may be the same. At the same time, our choices in life may not be the same, but to fight every battle coming our way, we must all know who we are. The more you understand and know who you are, the easier it is to ride through the seasons of your life.

The choices we make determine who we are. Our identity plays a role in understanding and executing our passion. Being a Christian is not a guarantee that we will receive all our heart's desires. Even though God wants us to receive all our desires, the devil constantly challenges us by setting traps so that we do not get to our destination. We must carry through our goals and never abandon them; we are to fight the battle with faith, wisdom and understanding. We will win, our goals fulfilled.

We have come to understand the essence of seasons, and we are grateful for this experience. In the everyday struggle to make things work, we figured out that we could choose to be happy now, seeing what we see and doing what we do. However, in many of the incidents in our adventure, things did not turn out how we desired. Therefore, I have wondered thus, *if we could change one thing to be happy during that phase, what would it be?* Given a chance, I will enjoy the lessons and put them into practice. I would appreciate life and the gift of living.

We must walk a season out, sacrificially and by faith. We cannot always trust our logical reasoning; no one knows what the future holds. Only God knows the aerial view of our life, the assignment on our lives and how we will come through. He knows the end from the beginning. We must stick to the view, the aerial view of that plan, if He allows us to get a glimpse of it. Moving forward demands that we take cognisance of the lessons learnt within this season; this is a one-off experience—an opportunity to grow and flourish.

We may have anticipated being happy in the next coming days, yet it may turn out to be a time of sadness and stress. This happens when God is pruning us and changing us. Having conceived this, we started to look for every reason to be grateful each day even though we have to fight through it. It took over nine months to realise this, but we decided to act immediately when we eventually did. Instead of being frustrated with our situation and those who have let us down, we reflected upon each day and acknowledged everything that went well.

We will always come across the different seasons; some are connected to us whilst others are linked to our extended family, friends, or neighbours; they will affect us regardless. Some seasons will take us from riches to rags, while others put us into places of new responsibilities. Some seasons can be impacted by health, financial or a change of circumstances. Whatever the season, the stronger you stand in your faith, the easier it will be to flow through those seasons. Many seasons will leave lasting marks of either pain, sorrow, or happiness. We must look out for others, offer a listening ear, be selfless, care less for money, and be as genuine as possible. There is always someone looking out to trust us to help them move forward. So let us use our passion to help and support others. Together we can........ if only for a season.

We will never remain the same once we have been through certain seasons, but there will be an opportunity to forgive and forget. Life seasons have the power to transform our moods; they change our perspectives and shift our lives. We can choose to stand still and be spectators, or we can choose to change and be transformed too. Whatever unpleasant experiences we went through can be forgiven and forgotten. We must choose to take positive action on our struggles and turn them into our passion to make changes.

Think through times

> *"Patience is bitter, but its fruit is sweet."*
> JEAN-JACQUES ROUSSEAU

Patience is a difficult virtue; it is a level of capacity people have before they get disheartened. Many people are not patient; they may be ignorant of what it entails to be patient. Some people may be tolerant, but it doesn't last long, and they give up midway. They need to understand why things are happening the way they are. As they maintain calmness, they will find patience and grace for the process and the lessons they are experiencing. Sometimes our patience may have been directed for a specific purpose, yet we may find it difficult to contain.

In some cases, our patience endures to the end. We all need a certain level of tolerance with our goals, even though it's not going to be easy. We must learn to accept setbacks, stand firm and acknowledge challenging situations without anger. My family experienced every bitterness during our journey, but we are now enjoying the fruits. We have learnt to be brave, to endure and wait patiently.

When we fight a good fight, we come through triumphant winners with all kinds of gains. Our suffering in any season ignites the zeal to do more, be kind and give to others. Once we have received grace through suffering, we also receive the grace to share and show love to others in times of poverty. The grace we received is not for us alone; neither is it for showing off. Barb Walters challenged us to *"share our kindness with the world and see what happens."*

We must learn to excel in our passion, whether in giving, showing compassion or other acts. In 2 Corinthians 8, Paul commended the church on their willingness to give regardless of how much they gave. The people of Corinth did not look at what they were going through, but they considered the difficult seasons experienced by others and acted. There was no hiding and no secrets; they expressed love by taking wholehearted action. They remembered others.

Giving does not always come in material value; we can share ideas too. Our success in achieving life goals is also measured by how we act and move forward to impact others. We must always excel in faith, love, knowledge and giving.

We must embark on our life journeys well equipped with the knowledge of the previous seasons and how the different seasons work. This helps us work on our inner self while nature does its part on the outside. We must, however, derive meaning from each season we go through and apply the lessons to our own lives. Everything happens for a reason. One may go through a double season in one year, whilst others experience treble. After all, life can never be the same for everyone.

Some seasons are short, whilst others last long, but all are symbolic; we must take a leaf out of each one. God created each season for us to live, learn and grow out of them. Similarly, God brings seasons for us to take a mental analysis. The onus lies with us. Your seasons in life may not follow the flow and time that nature does. Your seasons with the lessons you need will come to you when they are meant to come. You may feel like you are in your spring season when nature is in its autumn season. You may like the barren winter season when you are amid natures bountiful summer season. Your seasons flow as they are meant to flow.

We must understand what each season brings forth:

- Springtime brings restoration and rebirth.

- Autumn brings a time of shedding and releasing, which is preparing for progression through rest and restoration.

- Summer brings light and fruition, which may expose some of the mysteries that puzzled us. And when the light comes, we are exposed to a period of giving, sharing, and freeing ourselves to the light of life. This is knowledge and awareness.

- *"In winter, the earth sleeps; her creatures retreat" (Avia Woods).* Winter is usually the most wondrous and vivid one. It may look like nothing happens. But, for us God's people, winters are phases of opening, rallying, and going back to the background of what is meaningful. It is a time of peace and reflection.

There will be seasons of struggling or pain, but this should not deter us from planning our life. We must not forget to choose how we want to experience our seasons; abundance comes from expression. Milton Kamwendo inspires us to "think like a man of action and act like a man of thought"........ doing everything we have to do.

- What season are you going through now?

- Does it feel like a glorious one, or are you frustrated and scared?

- What do you hear? Or What do you see in your season?

Remember, as a child of God, you will never walk alone. At any moment in any season, you can turn to God to ask Him for support and guidance. Please remember that He does not always answer "now"; He allows you time to prepare for changes, but He is listening, and He will deliver at the perfect time for you. The more you choose to be still and listen, the more comfort and strength you will feel.

And it is, after all, only for a season.

Deuteronomy 30:15 says, *"Now listen, I am giving you a choice between life and death, between prosperity and disaster."* Verse 19 of the same chapter of Deuteronomy ends with *"So choose life in order that you may live, you and your offspring.*" (NIV). How amazing it is to know that we have options, life, or death. We all want to live; we all want to be successful. So, are we going to act or perish? My family chose to act and maintained humility.

One weekend we got into a hardware store and stumbled upon a little book of gratitude. We bought it, and from that day, we began to review our days and weeks. My husband calls it *our magic book;* it has sub-headings on gratitude, action plans, and daily events. We added these to our times of prayer. It was a great way to acquire skills for planning our lives. All this in one season; it has been a wonderful experience which we can walk through again if possible.

> *For with God, all things are possible.*
>
> (MATTHEW 19:26).

As we look forward to the future, we can effectively prepare for our life ahead. We have entered a new season. We are grateful that what appeared to be a setback turned into a setup, and there is now an abundance of rain. Doing things wrong may turn out to be a practical course in life.

God is powerful and awesome in the way He works. He will do things according to His time. Our failures save us well when they teach us valuable lessons. Everything we encountered during our winter season has given birth to amazing testimonies in our life. These are testimonies of meeting new friends, acquiring new skills, and carving our characters for the better. More importantly, God set us up to acquire a beautiful home within our means.

Having gone through all this, we would like to encourage anyone who finds themselves having a challenging round in life and feels like they are stuck in a challenging season to keep going. For there are some good times ahead. Take some time to grow from within and pray. God will hear your prayers.

You have what you need to grow through and achieve what you are destined to achieve. When you take each action step, God will show you the next one. Choose to be still and listen and you will know the right step to take. Remember to stay calm and offer praises and work on your regrets. Now is your turn to seize the moment and enjoy the experience of going through your opportunity. Wherever you are, enjoy the experience of going through your journey, Live, Learn, Grow. I wish you all the peace and happiness within your season so that you too, will become the person you're destined to be. Enjoy your seasons of creating life foundations.

If you know someone who does not understand the season they are going through in their life, please pass this book on.

I wish you well.

Let us pray

Father God, I thank you that you work through seasons.

You brought us this far to shower us with blessings.

Thank you for encouraging me to share my story in For a Season Live Learn Grow.

And for loving us and protecting us during the difficult phases of our lives.

Every season has brought rain to us, showers, hailstorms, and sometimes dark clouds.

We appreciate each period we have been through,

In this season, you have turned drought into an abundance of rain.

We receive the rain, the living waters, and the sunshine.

We are grateful the season has transformed us.

They have made us strong, and we experience happiness.

We give thanks for every learning experience.

We rejoice in the growth we see in our lives.

Thank you for your love, grace, and strength.

May your glory continue to be manifested through our testimonies.

May peace be with us now and forevermore,

Amen.

Acknowledgements

I want to acknowledge the Almighty who gives life and sustains humanity through all seasons; I could not have written and published this book without Him in my life.

I appreciate my wonderful husband, Richard, and our daughter Claire for their unwavering support; I am encouraged by how you humbled yourself and persevered through the difficult season we went through. You give me strength each day, and I feel proud to be a wife and mother. I am grateful for you and love you always.

To you, our incredible friends who put us up during a very challenging time in our lives. I wish you nothing else but that you may be blessed with abundance as you have given much. I can't thank you enough, Caroline Mapara- you are unique, fearfully, and wonderfully made. Thank you for your love, support, and patience with us. You gave us great inspiration; we shall be eternally grateful.

Thank you to great friends Jill and Steve. You showed us that one could forsake everything to give love, genuinely. Thank you for embracing us and walking with us through our season- true exemplary Christians.

Thank you to Dawn Chrystal for writing the foreword of this book. You are an inspiration and a role model. I am humbled to have met you.

Special thank you to selfless friends Tizza Douwona, Locadia Takawira and Dadirai Chekera. The prayers, the sacrifice and love, I don't know how to repay. May the Heavenly Father remember you when you call unto Him.

To my brother Fidelis Katehwe and Sister Imelda thank you for the inspiration and for being family. I look up to you.

Thank you to my church pastors Ian and Rachel; you have always been my supporters in every milestone. Thank you for fathering me in my faith.

To my Book coach and mentor, Vonayi Nyamazana, this project would not have been a success without you. Your insights and expertise are next to none. I have learnt, I have laughed, I have lived and grown. Thank you.

To my photographer Franco Sim photography and Book designer Sherman Baloyi, thank you for the beautiful images. You are a great team to work with.

To all the wonderful friends, every Transformational Coach around me, I treasure all of you. You are unique in your different ways, always there when I need you. Thank you for your inspirational guidance and support.

About the Author

Rujeko Oscars-Brown is a certified International Life Coach, NLP Practitioner, Entrepreneur and Motivational Speaker. She has a wealth of experience working with charities and voluntary organisations, and the education sector within the UK and Africa.

Rujeko's passion is in helping people unleash their potential to become the best of themselves, whether in their career, business, or relationships. As a personal success and empowerment coach, Rujeko helps people make decisions about their lives from fresh perspectives.

She is a holder of multiple degrees in Public Policy, Project Management, Educational Effectiveness and Housing Development. Half her life has been spent in the United Kingdom, having enjoyed the earlier half in Zimbabwe where she was born. Her experience working in the development sector with charities and voluntary organisations equips her with the values and ethics of diversity. She works with all genders and cultures though most of her work has been with women.

Now coaching full-time to individuals and groups, she facilitates meetings, group workshops and speaks to diverse audiences on empowerment, incremental growth and success.

Rujeko lives in Yorkshire, the UK, with her husband Richard and daughter Claire.

Contacts:
admin@mindamplification.com
WhatsApp: +447586904105 | +447375054284

Glossary of Terms

Budget - Financial plan, money, or cost.

Chain - several linked property sales. In a chain, the exchange of contracts must take place together.

Comfort zone - a temperature range within which one is comfortable. A certain level in a situation where one functions well or within ease.

Completion Date - the day when all monies, documents and transactions relating to a house have been distributed.

Covid-19 Pandemic - a disease caused by infection with severe acute respiratory syndrome coronavirus strain.

Contract - An agreement between the buyer and seller.

Conveyancer - a person other than a solicitor or lawyer who is involved in carrying all legal work relating to buying or selling of properties.

Financial promises of God - Covenants or declarations made by God concerning financial blessing on his people.

Fittings and Fixtures - every non-structural item included in the purchase of a house.

Furloughed - to be laid off work.

Home Buyers Report - A summary detailing the structural condition of most parts of the property which are accessible.

House Viewings - a time to look around eligible properties.

House buyer - the person buying a house or home.

Lockdown - an emergency where people are not allowed to enter, leave, or move around freely. Lockdown can be offered by police or government.

Estate agents - companies whose jobs are for selling, renting, or buying buildings for clients.

Nutrient deficiencies - when body doesn't get enough nutrients from food. Deficiencies can lead to different health problems.

Property ladder - stage one to go through in owning a house. It can be from a flat to a mansion.

Plan B - second option or something that can be acted upon when preferred method fails.

Psalmist - The author of the book of psalm or composer of a psalm.

Rhema word - God's word spoken specifically to an individual.

Seasons of life - The times we experience for different purpose in life.

Searches - Checks carried on the property from the local council records for planning. applications, restrictions, and covenants.

Stamp Duty - Tax paid to the government by the buyer upon house purchase completion.

Soft furnishings - Items or fabrics used in the home.

Survey - an inspection carried by a qualified surveyor.

Title Deeds - legal documents showing ownership of a property or piece of land.

Under Offer - The seller has accepted an offer on the property however contracts have not yet been signed.

Vendor - a person selling a house or house seller.

Help and Information for Homebuyers

1. **Financial Conduct Authority UK**- https://www.fca.org.uk/firms/mortgage-lenders-intermediaries.

2. **Bank of England Mortgages**- https://www.bankofengland.co.uk/.

3. **Money Saving Expert**- https://www.moneysavingexpert.com/mortgages/buying-a-home-timeline/.

4. **UKGovernment**- How to buy a Home- https://www.gov.uk/government/publications/how-to-buy-a-home/how-to-buy.

5. **Mortgages Regulation UK**- https://assets.publishing.service.gov.uk/government/uploads/system/uploads/attachment_data/file/81508/consult_mortgage_regulation.pd.

6. **The National Association of Estate Agents**-Upholding good practice- https://www.ukecc-services.net/naea.cfm.

7. **UK Association of Letting Agents**- https://www.ukala.org.uk/.

8. **RICS**- Royal Institution of Chartered Surveyors- - https://www.rics.org/uk/ .

9. **RICS Home Buyer Survey**- https://www.localbuildingsurveyor.co.uk/?gclid=EAIaIQobChMI_YWAs_qu8gIVFp7VCh3OGg-ZlEAAYAiAAEgJVk_D_BwE.

10. **Residential Property Surveyors Association**- https://www.localsurveyorsdirect.co.uk/residential-property-surveyors-association-rpsa.

11. **Property mark**- The professional body for the property sector-https://www.propertymark.co.uk/.

12. **Citizen's Advice UK**- https://www.citizensadvice.org.uk/.

13. **Home stratosphere**- Everything about the home- https://www.citizensadvice.org.uk/.

14. **Rightmove**- Properties for sale or to rent in the UK- https://www.rightmove.co.uk/.

15. **Zoopla**- Houses to rent or for sale.

16. **Your Move**- House Buying Process in the UK- https://www.your-move.co.uk/buy/guides/house-buying-process-england-and-wales.

17. **Your move**- Information and Property Valuation- https://www.your-move.co.uk/.

18. **Boomin**- Properties from UK Estate Agents- https://www.boomin.com/.

19. **UK Estate Agents**- https://www.home.co.uk/search/agents/.

20. **Mortgages Online UK**- https://mortgages.online/articles/mortga .